NOT TOO FRAYED TO FLY

Surviving the loss of your soul mate

NOT TOO FRAYED TO FLY

Surviving the loss of your soul mate

Betts McCalla

Running Quail Press

USA

Running Quail Press, Inc.
www.runningquailpress.com

Name: McCalla, Betts
Title: Not Too Frayed to Fly | Betts McCalla
Identifiers: ISBN 978-0-9862708-8-8 | ISBN 978-0-9862708-9-5 (ebook)
Author photo: www.photosbyleanna.com
Excerpts reprinted by permission © From Grief to Peace, LLC, 2016, www.FromGriefToPeace.org

Printed in the United States of America

For Jerry, for all time

"To everything there is a season, a time for
every purpose under heaven: a time to weep,
and a time to laugh; a time to mourn, and a
time to dance."
Ecclesiastes 3:1,4

Table of Contents

Acknowledgments

I'd like to thank Joy Collins and Cathy Marley for your invaluable insights and inspiration, warm hugs, and "shoulders" shared during our weekly writers' meetings. Thank you, Desert Ridge Barnes & Noble Booksellers and Renee, for your kind hospitality and perfect setting for our creative minds.

To my tireless editor and best sister-friend, Clelia (Clo) Brickley, thanks for your help in polishing this manuscript and for always having my back. I want to thank Bonnie Fatio, founder of AgeEsteem®, for writing the best foreword I could have imagined and for sharing valuable contacts.

Long before I found my soul mate, Jerry, I had six people in my life that protected, encouraged, loved, and accepted me. My mother, Jean, worked two jobs but taught us right from wrong, never left home without kissing us goodbye, got us to church, and made sure we got good grades. Her love and devotion never wavers. My three sisters, Melody, Clelia, and Debbie, and two brothers, James and Chuck, cheered me on and cheered me up. You were my built-in best friends and playmates. I will always love you all.

Foreword by Bonnie Fatio

Not Too Frayed to Fly is a must read whether you have just lost a loved one and are seeking to understand what it means for the rest of your life, or whether you are still with a partner and wish to be prepared for the moment when one of you will remain alone.

Through my work with AgeEsteem®, I have interviewed people around the world about their views on age and aging. Their stories often express the emptiness and fear of being alone. Death takes an important toll on the living. When your loved one dies, something within you dies also. Your world crashes, your confidence shatters, your sense of self shrinks, and your identity disappears. Yet you continue to breathe.

On a recent flight home from speaking at a conference in Oslo, Norway, I chatted with the woman in the seat next to mine. She explained that most of her friends no longer dared travel alone at age seventy. She had been widowed eight years earlier and chose to travel abroad alone to visit friends. When I told her about *Not Too Frayed to Fly*, she immediately took out her iPhone to preorder it. Just as the book resonated with her, I think it will also speak to you.

Betts McCalla takes us on a rollercoaster ride with her as she bounces from grief—to overwhelmingly joyous memories—to what you need to know to survive. From the opening words that she kept repeating to herself, "You're scared. You are going to be okay. He's dead. You're not dead," I was caught up in the power of her naked soul as she shared all that matters.

Betts McCalla invites us into the intimacy of

her heart and thoughts. We are introduced to Jerry, her soul mate and spouse, sharing their special story. Whatever the memory, it somehow connects you to Betts and Jerry, drawing you into their unique loving relationship. Little things become enormously important. She teases us to laugh and cry with her as she shares her journey from being a wet body of tears to seeking how to live without Jerry while still feeling his presence.

Hers is a story of bravery and humor as she takes control and drives through the United States to rediscover life. It is also a story of restoration, moving from total devastation to a new wholeness.

Amidst all this are savory tips for each of us. What to do and what not to do. She warns and informs us of scams that prey on those who are weak with grief. She advises us on how we can best help the friend who has lost a spouse. She guides us through steps to reclaim our "self." She challenges us and inspires us, offering herself as a role model.

For my husband of fifty-two years and me, conversations to prepare for the future are common. Such discussions are essential as we grow older. When I reached Betts McCalla's checklist in "Chapter Three, First 30 Days Financial Work," I told my husband, "We need to read this together." Betts has given us a treasure trove of information we don't really want to deal with, yet we must. It is invaluable. This is the time to prepare, now when we are together and both healthy. The book has inspired many a conversation with family and friends, also. The death of a partner is a reality of the life cycle. We cannot ignore the certainty of death. Yet we are never quite prepared for the finality of it. Nor do we foresee the stress of finding our way around a mountain of paperwork when we are fraught with endless emotion.

Not Too Frayed to Fly is a gift to the world. Each of us will benefit from reading this book. It is the story of grief, memories of precious moments and joyous living, questioning what is next, and hope. It is for those who have lost a loved one and those who wish to be prepared.

Bonnie Fatio, founder, AgeEsteem

Bonnie Fatio is a master change catalyst and global speaker. She has held leadership roles in business, local government, civic groups, and the international community.

Most recently she founded Inspired Women Lead, a global cross-border, cross-culture mentoring movement to help women step into their authentic feminine power as leaders. Each woman who is personally mentored, then mentors another woman. Today inspired women in 35 countries are being mentored to lead globally, and over 1,000,000 lives are being impacted.

www.BonnieFatio.com

Introduction

You're scared. You are going to be okay. He's dead. You're not dead. These four sentences kept repeating in my head the first few days after Jerry passed. Sometimes you feel that you have searched harder than imaginable and still cannot find what you're looking for. I felt that way for a very long time after my husband transitioned. I needed answers to practical questions as well as finite ones.

All my life, I've been a student. Whenever I encounter a problem, I research it until I find a workable solution. When my soul mate passed, I expected to quickly find the answer to "What do I do next?" There were tons of online articles written by accounting and investment firms offering financial advice to those recently widowed. I also found many generic grief books that I couldn't relate to. What I needed was advice from a grieving spouse whose heart had just been destroyed and whose mind was only able to grasp rational thoughts for minutes at a time. So many answers eluded me. I had gut-wrenching, heartbreaking, and brain-throbbing questions that I desperately needed answered. I had lost my best friend, my lover, my spouse, my soul mate, my cheerleader, and the only person who accepted me unconditionally, scars and all. What was I supposed to do? How was I supposed to act? I wanted to rip at my clothes and pull out my hair. I wanted to wail and shriek. Normally, I was the calm one who could always be counted on in a crisis. Now, I bounced from a state of manic activity to being totally withdrawn, often in the space of an hour.

I needed to sleep, but sleep was denied. I had slept upright in a recliner next to my husband's hospital bed the last sixty days of his life, snatching naps that rarely lasted more than an hour at a time. I had forgotten how to sleep in a bed, and I sure as hell didn't know how to sleep alone. And, damn it, I didn't want to learn. I started listening to books on tape so I could fall asleep. To this day, I still cannot sleep without earbuds and a book on tape.

I spent the next several months after his death, tackling problems and navigating through fog. I needed a step-by-step, to do list upon the death of a soul mate. I felt like I had a fatal, rapidly advancing and physically overwhelming disease called grief, and I desperately needed to find the cure. Combing through bookstores, I bought anything that sounded promising. I could not find what I needed in one book or five books or even twenty to help me proceed through my grief in an orderly fashion. I was bereft, and part of my soul had been taken away—the best part. The Jerry part of JerryandBetts or BettsandJerry was missing—the part that held my sweetest essence. I feared my capacity to love had vanished. I needed someone to share the intimate details of widowhood with me—a how-to manual or survival kit written for someone like me—a person who had lost her soul mate, her lifeline.

This is the book I wish I had found. I'm writing it to help you. A book like this might have assuaged some of my irrational fears. It might have propped up my ego and made me aware that although I was no longer part of a unit of two equaling one, I was still a functioning unit. It could have allowed me to lie down knowing my love might come and comfort me in my dreams with a light touch. It certainly would have made me less afraid of the years to come. This book is a love story but not a fairy tale. It gives practical advice and suggestions while sharing the intimacy of mine and Jerry's relationship. It will help get you through the early stages of loss and encourage you to move forward, seek out other people who have lost their soul mates, share lessons learned, and exchange heart hugs. This book may inspire you to watch for possible signs from your soul mate or loved one who has passed. And, above all, it may empower you to find yourself again and not be too frayed to fly. Your journey from grief to peace begins now.

Chapter One
Soul Mates Forever

This is the story of the love we shared that death cannot change.

That last night, my sister and I encircled Jerry in a tight embrace as he sat upright in his bed at the hospice facility and gazed directly past us at something we couldn't see. We each held one of his hands, telling him we loved him and knew he was leaving. We lied and said we were going to be okay. His body was so hot—it felt like a rocket getting ready to launch—and then he squeezed our hands, and his spirit took off. Cause of death was metastatic lung cancer.

During the short months of his fatal illness, I asked him how he would contact me once he passed on. He replied that he wouldn't know what was allowed until he got to where he was going. But Jerry promised that if he could contact me, I would know it was him. At the time of his passing, I was like most of you—totally unsure of whether or not something happens after death. Based on religious teachings of my Protestant background, I had a basic concept that heaven was somewhere up in the sky, and we would all meet again someday with our loved ones who had passed (except of course those who were going to hell in a handbasket). Although this concept was somewhat reassuring, I needed an insight into how to sustain contact. Jerry was my soul mate, and my belief is that the connection cannot be severed.

Early in our relationship, we expressed that we felt we had known each other forever. As time went on, Jerry and I grew to believe we were soul mates and that we had been together in other lifetimes. We were amazed with the similarities in our thoughts and viewpoints, considering that our upbringing and backgrounds (up until the point when we met) were light years apart. We could finish each other's thoughts and sentences almost from day one. Nothing in Jerry's or my past would have indicated we were destined to meet, but all it took was a brief encounter on the one day I visited the city where he lived, Minneapolis. I believe in kismet. I believe in miracles. And I know soul mates exist.

Immediately after Jerry's passing, he began to make his continued presence known to me and to my sister, Clo. When we mentioned his name, we would often hear a noise in the kitchen; it was usually the sound of the plastic cover being knocked off the trash can. We would say, "Hi Jerry," and a feeling of warmth and peace would come over us.

29

Betts McCalla

When we least expected it, he tossed us bright shiny pennies that magically appeared throughout the house, outside on the sidewalk, or next to our car doors. It wasn't until much later that I realized there were probably many signs from him that went unnoticed.

Chapter Two
Our Stories

Jerry was the youngest of three children and quite a surprise baby being twelve years younger than his closest sibling. His middle-class parents were in their forties when he was conceived, and his mother suffered terribly from debilitating rheumatoid arthritis disease. Jerry grew up in Pennsylvania, helping and caring for his mother and baking bread at his father's bakery. He sang with a band and was part of the wrestling team at school. After graduating from high school, he joined the United States Air Force. Not making spy school because he lacked the necessary MacGyver aptitude, Jerry was trained to be a medic. After a severe head injury and prolonged recovery, he was discharged. Returning home to Pennsylvania to attend college, he married his high school sweetheart and started a family. And they moved to Minnesota.

My parents were both nineteen the year I was born. Mom was a bookkeeper at a shoe factory in Little Rock, Arkansas. Her parents were local farmers. She had that beautiful Ingrid Bergman look. My dad was in the Army. He was a singer, one-quarter American Indian, and from the area in New York City known as Hell's Kitchen. They met at a United Service Organizations (USO) dance, fell in love, and married. When dad was transferred, mom stayed in Arkansas.

When I was two and a half years old, I contracted polio, was paralyzed from the neck down, and spent months in an iron lung. My mother was young, and the doctors told her I should be placed in a long-term care facility because I would remain a "basket case" and would never be able to take care of myself, work, marry, or have a normal life. Mama took me home. There were two types of treatment used for polio patients. The first was the Sister Kenny method, which involved lots of hot compresses with wet woolen cloths cut from Army blankets along with stretching and massage. The other method involved braces. To this day, the scent of wet wool makes me nauseous. Arkansas was primarily a brace state. Placing me in a full leg brace at the age of three gave necessary support to my partially paralyzed leg so I could walk again; however, it apparently stunted the growth of my leg, causing a measurable discrepancy in length. My mother massaged my limbs daily and took me for physical therapy three times a week. I remember having whirlpool treatments in a round metal vat up to my neck in hot swirling water.

My father came home from the service and

got a job selling life insurance, but he knew in his heart he was a singer. To advance my father's singing career, my parents moved to Chicago. Five more children were added to the family as my parents struggled with my father's alcoholism and the ups and downs of a performer's life.

At twelve years old when my parents divorced, I became the surrogate mother to my siblings and the main sounding board for my single-parent mother. Money was incredibly tight. Mom worked two jobs most of the time, and no help was ever received from my father. From the age of nine until I was sixteen, I had years of ongoing medical treatments for the residual damage from polio, including seven corrective surgeries involving muscle transplants, leg-lengthening procedures, and two spinal fusions, which required spending a year in a full body cast. This is how I usually spent my summer vacations.

Following one of the surgeries, I was given

either mismatched or tainted blood. My temperature rose to 105, and I was trembling all over when my mother arrived for her daily visit. She took one look at me and started screaming for help. The nurses packed me in ice to reduce my fever, and I had an out-of-body experience. My spirit remained in the hospital room hovering over my bed, watching my body being worked on and seeing my mother's gray complexion. She saved my life by arriving when she did. The next day, she told my brothers and sisters how scary it had been and that they had almost lost me. This was my first brush with death. My surgeries were paid for mostly by the March of Dimes foundation along with whatever my mom could contribute. From an early age, I learned to navigate the medical field and to ask questions. I became very comfortable communicating with adults and dealing with medical personnel. And I developed a lifelong passion for reading and research.

Jerry and I met the spring after I turned twenty-three. I worked for a graphic design company and was awarded my first bona fide business trip, traveling from Chicago, where I lived, to visit my firm's new branch office in Minneapolis. After spending the day with the branch manager, a friend of his named Jerry stopped into the office to say hello. I was staying overnight with some friends who had recently relocated from Chicago. Because my friends lived close to Jerry's neighborhood, and the branch manager lived in the opposite direction, Jerry offered to drop me off. Jerry and I fell into intense like that first day we met. There was lots of bantering, flirting, and interesting conversation. I considered him good-looking, intelligent, sexy, and blessedly safe. He was married, thirty-two years old, and the father of four. I enjoyed my single life and had no plans for long-term relationships or a family until I was much older. I did not have any good role models for marriage. My grandparents were separated. My parents were divorced. My aunt and uncle were divorced. As the eldest of six children, I had spent most of my childhood being responsible for my siblings. I was finally living alone and loving it. I had a great job, a spacious four-room apartment with two closets, and a bathroom all to myself.

Over the next year, Jerry and his wife separated. He and I became best friends and then lovers. Eventually he moved to Chicago, and we started a business together.

Fast forward three and a half years: As married business partners, we lived in downtown Chicago in a high-rise building with a view of Lake Michigan. Every other weekend, we commuted to Minneapolis to share custody of Jerry's four children with his ex-wife. We worked and lived together 24/7 and never ran out of things to talk about. It was like we needed to catch up on the years we had spent without each other.

In Chicago, we formed several companies

and worked side by side doing television and film production. It was a challenging and exciting industry. We were given the opportunity to produce a five-night/week syndicated television talk show called *Underground News.* The show featured interviews with newsworthy personalities such as Jane Fonda, Woody Allen, Charles Percy, Abbie Hoffman, Joan Baez, and John Lennon as well as musical performances by Harry Chapin, Jim Croce, and others. We also produced a documentary series hosted by actor Peter Lawford and a music show called *Dig It, Electric Sight and Sound* that was the precursor for simulcast musical programming.

To become more involved in Jerry's children's lives, we relocated to Minneapolis. His two oldest sons came to live with us during their turbulent teenage years, and I got my first gray hairs. Later we were offered an opportunity to relocate to California to grow our businesses. We had visited California the previous winter, and there was no way I was passing on a chance to move away from snow and ice. Although the original opportunity was short-lived, we expanded our careers in other directions. Jerry became a therapist and eventually opened a clinic specializing in pain management. I went to work for and subsequently purchased (with three other employees) an aftermarket manufacturing company in the automotive industry.

When Jerry and I were together, we felt we were invincible and a family. We were each other's best friend, lover, and confidante, and that made our world complete. I learned to love camping and fishing and the state of Hawaii. We indulged those interests while spending our vacations in beautiful locales like Big Sur, California; Sedona, Arizona; Whistler, BC in Canada; and the island of Kauai. We were often able to add play days onto the end of trade shows in fun locales. Clo, my sister, lived with us for several years and usually accompanied us on our camping vacations. She and I counted on Jerry to prepare a scrumptious dinner for us each evening over the Coleman stove and the campfire. One afternoon, Jerry decided to walk along the Big Sur river and "wet a line." It was a kind of drizzly, cool day, which was common in northern California on the ocean, and Jerry was gone a long time.

It had just gotten dark when he showed up at the campsite, driven back by a new friend. He explained that he had ended up miles downriver because that was where the fish were biting. He said he had caught his dinner, and when we asked where his stringer was, he proceeded to flip several fish out of the pockets of his beautiful new Bemidji wool jacket.

We came up with the phrase "pocket trout" to indicate small fish. My sister was unhappy because she had been using his jacket as an extra layer of covers during the cold nights, and now it smelled too fishy to bring into the tent.

People often paint a glossy perfect picture of someone after they have passed. Jerry and I did share a magical life together. One of our friends likened our lifestyle to being on vacation every day. I think she was referring to our many mini-vacations, the apparent lack of stress in our lives, our constant bantering back and forth, and the friendship it was easy to see we enjoyed whenever and wherever we were together. It was a sweet life between us. In the entire scope of our thirty-five-year relationship, I only remember three major disagreements—not fights but disagreements. They all involved my wanting to bring home yet another warm, wiggly puppy or cuddly kitten to add to our menagerie. Jerry didn't like small yappy dogs and would always come up with reasons we should avoid them, such as they pass gas, they tend to nip, or they are too fragile. As soon as I brought home my next "I can't live without" critter, this newest addition would worm its way into his heart within

41

hours. Truth be told, he was a complete mush when it came to domestic animals of all sizes, including horses.

Jerry was my best friend, my strongest supporter, the president of my fan club, and the true love of my life. And I know I was his. His face would light up whenever I came into a room, and he made me laugh every day. The two of us were a self-sustaining unit, and we were usually on a roll.

We took lots of classes together: Japanese language because we planned on visiting Kyoto (one of Jerry's favorite cities), Thai cuisine, transactional analysis, and pot throwing. Once I signed us up for a juggling class because it sounded like fun. It was too much for my physical limitations, but Jerry loved it and would often juggle small items as he walked around his office—much to the amusement of his practitioners and the patients in the waiting room. We worked hard at our businesses, earning some success from our individual endeavors, and life was good. We joined a local Presbyterian church and did some volunteer work. We enjoyed spending time with and making memorable meals for our eclectic collection of friends and our extended family, but we loved it even more when it was just the two of us, eating grilled-cheese sandwiches and cream of tomato soup from trays in front of the fireplace.

There were physical bumps in the road like my sustaining a bad fall, which resulted in a shattered tibia, detached peroneal tendon, and fractured hip. Healing from the fractures took over a year. This was the precursor to the onset of post-polio syndrome for me. Post-polio syndrome is an illness of the nervous system usually triggered by a major trauma to the body and can appear fifteen to fifty years after you've had polio. It affects your muscles and nerves and causes you to have weakness, fatigue, and muscle and joint pain. Day-to-day activities become more difficult to perform.

You are often so exhausted by the end of the day that it's an effort not to fall asleep over your dinner plate. I had to learn to conserve my energy and to lean on Jerry more. We adapted our lifestyle to accommodate my needs. Jerry took over doing the laundry and our grocery shopping and did most of the cooking. Fortunately, he was an excellent cook and loved to experiment. He credited his culinary talent to his father who was a professional baker and chef, and to his Swedish mother.

The first Christmas Jerry and I were together, I got a taste of his Swedish heritage. He announced that we were going to make Christmas cookies and needed to go shopping for ingredients. I knew I was in over my head when he placed eight pounds of unsalted butter into the shopping cart. He had a special little hand-cranked cookie press he used to form the spritz cookies into shapes of Christmas trees, ornaments, and wreaths. He made dozens of butter-ladened spritz, sandbakkels, and fattigmann cookies while entertaining me with childhood stories like when his mama made cookies and let him use the cookie press to play streetcar conductor. Naturally, Jerry demonstrated to me all the physicality that role demanded along with sound effects. My contribution was baking many small loaves of banana-nut bread and cooking several batches of fudge. Every year we made up trays of homemade goodies for our family, friends, and close business associates. People professed to staying friends with us just for Jerry's Christmas cookies.

We were together thirty-one years when Jerry called me at the office one afternoon to say he thought he was having a heart attack and was driving himself to the hospital. He made it to the ER before suffering a massive heart attack. After running a few tests, the attending cardiologist recommended immediate quadruple bypass surgery. Jerry had the surgery the following morning. While in the Intensive Care Unit (ICU) right after the surgery, both his lungs collapsed. His physicians placed him in a medically induced coma, and he remained in ICU for three weeks. He contracted a severe bacterial infection called MRSA (Methicillin-Resistant Staphylococcus Aureus), and we visitors had to put on yellow protective gowns and face masks before we could enter his hospital room. As his advocate, I stayed at the hospital 24/7. I was terrified that if I turned my back for a minute, Jerry would die. One night, I ran out of cash for the cafeteria, and the cashiers didn't accept credit or debit cards. I stood in front of an Automated Teller Machine (ATM) and realized I didn't even know our code or how to use the machine. I was so used to going to the bank for money, and Jerry was the one who would access an ATM if we needed it. I found the code in Jerry's wallet—it was my birthdate—I should have known.

By the time Jerry was brought out of his

coma and able to breathe again on his own, he had developed Sundowner's Syndrome, which made him so paranoid he couldn't be left alone. We discovered his trauma had caused him to forget how to even sign his name. In addition to heart disease, he was diagnosed with Chronic Obstructive Pulmonary Disease (COPD). He refused to go to a rehabilitation center and insisted he had to come home. Our wonderful friends, Marcia, a physical therapist, and her husband Al came from southern California to Arizona and stayed with us for a week. Then Jerry's daughter Stephanie visited for a few weeks and worked hard helping him gain enough strength to walk outside first to the mailbox and then to the corner of our street and back.

We kept up a round-robin rotation of our guest room for months so that someone would be at home with Jerry. He spent hours every day learning to write again. Six weeks later, he started cardiac rehabilitation, and we began the "chicken" phase of our lives. Jerry loved beef but was on a mission to get healthy again, so steak became a thing of the past replaced by chicken or turkey for every lunch or dinner meal. These are two of my least favorite foods followed only by liver and fish. We resumed a normal though slightly restricted lifestyle. I dreamed of steak and loaded baked potatoes.

Jerry's miraculous recovery and the ensuing three years felt like bonus time to us. We began taking a four-day mini-vacation every month to spend even more time together. We felt we had come through fire and survived. Jerry completed writing his first novel, and after it was published, he started working on a sequel. One of the highlights after completing his novel was attending his fiftieth high school reunion in Pennsylvania and presenting a copy of his book to his ninety-one-year-old English teacher. She kept saying, "I never thought Jerry would be the one to write a book." He got such a kick out of retelling that story. On the plane ride home, Jerry developed a nagging cough and started feeling signs of the flu with severe aching muscles and joint pain. A few days after he got home, I went into the hospital for a scheduled laminectomy. He coughed and coughed each time he came to visit me. I developed complications and kept running a fever. He said he felt exhausted, and I encouraged him not to make the ninety-mile roundtrip visit every day.

Earlier that year, Jerry had started having a lot of joint and muscle pain in his hands, arms, and hips. He was diagnosed with advanced rheumatoid arthritis. This was the hereditary disease that his mother had suffered with for years, and he always feared he would get it. Due to his increase in pain, his rheumatologist wanted to start him on a new drug. Before Jerry could receive it, his doctor required a chest X-ray and some blood work. About three weeks after my surgery, Jerry went for his X-ray. That same evening, his doctor called and said the radiologist had found a mass on his lung that looked like cancer. This resulted in frenzied efforts on our part to get a biopsy quickly scheduled after the referral from his pulmonologist indicated a four-to-six-week wait. We wanted an immediate "What stage is it?" diagnosis and to find the best treatment available in Phoenix.

I had recently used an outstanding diagnostic radiologist during a medical procedure of my own, and we were able to facilitate Jerry's biopsy through her. She performed the biopsy, prepared the slides, and hand-carried them through the hospital laboratory while we waited. We had the results immediately. Our lovely, blonde radiologist walked back into the procedure room after examining the aspirated sample of tissue she had removed minutes earlier from my husband's chest and reached for his hand. "Jerry, I'm really sorry. It's definitely cancer, non-small cell lung carcinoma to be exact, and from what I can see, it's inoperable." Cancer. That is one big ugly terrifying word. This was the confirmation we didn't want to hear. Jerry had been a health care professional so was able to ask the right questions. I just felt numb.

Through his network of friends and medical practitioners, Jerry quickly got an appointment at a leading cancer treatment center and was given a stage 2A diagnosis. The thoracic surgeons told us that if Jerry had surgery to remove the upper lobe of his diseased lung, then had radiation and chemotherapy treatments, he would probably live another two or perhaps two and a half years of good quality life. Without any treatment, he might live six months. Jerry wasn't ready to quit living. He believed in modern medicine, and he wanted to fight. We talked over the options, prayed about it, and he made his choice to have surgery, radiation treatments, and chemotherapy. A month later, the specialists removed the upper lobe of his left lung. It looked like they had removed half of his back. It was so concave.

As his illness progressed, our life together changed dramatically, but Jerry continued to be the sweet romantic man I loved. He insisted on taking me to Laughlin for a special Valentine's Day weekend. It turned into a very traumatic experience. Jerry got up to use the bathroom in the middle of the night, tripped over my power wheelchair, and fell and broke his nose. He ended up having to go to the emergency room to get it treated.

The next day Jerry was scheduled to start his radiation therapy. He only delayed it a day. And five weeks later, he began the chemo treatments. After the second round of chemo treatments, Jerry was so immunosuppressed that he developed shingles and couldn't stand anything confining against his skin. He had to borrow my cotton nightshirts for a couple of weeks. His favorite was a blue print with koi fish. Sometimes now when I wear it, I remember him commenting that only I would have an appropriate nightshirt for a fisherman. Somehow he managed to hang onto his sense of humor and continued to make me laugh. Nauseous, in pain, and fed up with all the rules being imposed on us, he turned to me one afternoon, and with a perfectly straight face said, "Have them bring my car around. I'm checking out of this flea-bag establishment." I burst into laughter. And once again I felt grounded.

Because Jerry had been the chef in our marriage, the kitchen was his domain. I prepared one or two meals a week at most before he became ill. We usually went out to dinner a couple of nights a week, and he would cook the other evenings. When we had dinner parties, he planned and prepared the appetizers and the main course. I was in charge of the salad and dessert.

Prior to his illness, I would go for days barely opening the refrigerator and only spending time in the kitchen doing the nightly clean up after dinner. When Jerry got sick, his appetite greatly changed, and he usually preferred comfort food like soup and sandwiches or pasta. I felt like an intruder in our kitchen for the eight months I prepared our nightly meals. The kitchen missed Jerry, and the pots and pans belonged to him. He had assembled the cookware and various utensils, and they were loyal to him. The utensils would hook themselves together so I would have to fumble through them trying to dislodge a ladle or whisk. A favorite wooden spoon he often used chose to break apart in my hand after I selected it. Food stuck to the pans when I cooked, getting scorched. And every knife I picked up seemed dull and intent on rejecting me. The spices were arranged in a chef-created jumble with the most used closest at hand; whereas, I tend to alphabetize them. None of the lids would fit the pans I selected. It was as though the kitchen conspired against me. I was an interloper, an amateur in its eyes, and it wanted the master back. Damn it, I wanted him back in the kitchen, too.

We kept faith and told each other this would soon be behind us, and we could continue with our lives. My darling got sicker and sicker as each week went by. The cancer was progressing and rapidly spread into his spine and pelvis. It skipped stage 3 and moved directly into stage 4. His pain was excruciating from bones fracturing in his spine and hips. I spent evenings swapping out his ice packs as he sought relief without resorting to mind-numbing drugs. We tried to find something to laugh about every day. He was my wonderful compassionate love, and I held on tight to him.

Jerry's first book had been published the month before his diagnosis. When he felt well enough, we worked on marketing his novel. He talked about his writing experience, answered questions (everyone has a book they want to write), and sold books to his healthcare professionals. I often walked into his hospital or hospice room, and he would hand me a check or a twenty-dollar bill that he had made from selling a book. Jerry had a larger-than-life personality and an incredible zest for living, which he shared with everyone. My mother always says, "Jerry never met a stranger."

He lived eight horrific, agonizing, and humbling months after his surgery. And I began my life as a widow. Now that I've shared my story, let's get to work.

Chapter Three
First 30 Days Financial Work

This is your checklist. You are probably thinking, "You've got to be kidding. Just leave me alone and let me pull the covers over my head and sob."

Okay, even though you feel numb and incapable of adding simple sums, you need to take care of steps 1 to 5 immediately. Then you can take some time to work on the rest of the list.

1. Start with gathering enough cash to cover immediate expenses for at least thirty days. It is critical to understand that accounts (including your joint bank accounts) could be

frozen for weeks once banks and credit card companies have been notified of the death. So you will need to make plans to prevent any hardship this might cause.

2. If you are employed, you will need to notify your manager of your loss. Most companies only allow a short bereavement period of three to five days. This time off is not covered by the Family and Medical Leave Act (FMLA). If you can handle it financially, request additional time off even if you must take it without pay. I returned to work after three weeks and found it incredibly hard to concentrate on business matters. A total of four or five weeks would have been so much better.

3. Request death certificates. The very first thing you will be asked to provide when making changes to banking information, applying for insurance benefits, and setting

up any legal claims will be a certified copy of the death certificate. You can usually order these through the funeral home or by contacting the Vital Statistics office in the state in which the death occurred. Go ahead and order twelve copies so that you have enough. Some recipients may accept a faxed copy, but most will require an original certified document. There will probably be a charge for each certified copy requested. I paid seven dollars each.

4. Locate the Will if there is one. This is especially important to determine if there are burial instructions or bequests that need to be followed immediately. Not all states require probate, and it is often determined by the asset valuation. If the deceased had a Will, he or she probably named an executor who will be in charge of carrying out final wishes and distributing property. If the person died

without a Will (also known as intestacy), state law typically provides a list of those who could serve in this capacity. It is important to note that property transferred at death is governed by state law, and the terms differ from state to state. If you are named executor, you should obtain Letters Testamentary, a document that provides proof that you have a right to handle the deceased's financial affairs during probate. You may want to consult an estate attorney to help you through the probate process.

5. Publish a brief obituary that lists the funeral home. Keep five copies of the newspaper, showing the date the obituary was published. This publication is sometimes required as proof of public notification. Obituaries often elicit condolences from friends and past acquaintances. But they also might garner solicitations from companies wanting to sell

you everything from home repairs, security systems, solar panels, annuities, insurance policies, reverse mortgages, and other investment opportunities. Just as there are lawyers who chase ambulances, there are service contractors who scour the obituaries. If you need these services, contract with reliable companies that you or someone you trust has a history with. Avoid sharing personal information like cause of death or times you plan to be away from home—the mortuary can be contacted for schedule details. Predators sometimes scan obituaries looking for opportunities to burglarize homes that have narcotic medications and will be empty for hours during visitation and funeral services. And speaking of predators, the week after my husband passed, someone attempted to break into my home through the back door. It was late at night, and I was in my wheelchair wearing a nightgown and folding my laundry. First, I heard loud footsteps as someone approached the back door, stepping onto the wooden wheelchair ramp. The predator had a clear view of my vulnerable state through the window, and I could hear the terrifying sound of the keylock being manipulated with some sort of tool. I picked up my cell phone to call the police, and the predator took off. He was long gone when the police arrived, and my terrific watchdogs were sound asleep in the bedroom. Very scary experience. If you live alone, consider any steps you should take to ensure your safety. I had an alarm system installed after that incident and some outdoor motion sensor lights.

6. Create a calendar showing the due dates of your bills, if you don't already have one. Make sure you pay the utility bills on or

before the due dates to avoid any interruption in service that could trigger a demand for an additional security deposit. Contact utility companies and other service providers to change the name on the account if necessary. Look over bank and credit card statements. Be aware of any automatic withdrawals that could cause an overdraft and trigger service fees. This is the preamble to preparing your budget. If you need to be cautious about expenditures, promptly identify and cancel any unnecessary monthly recurring charges, such as gym memberships, club membership dues, digital subscriptions for Netflix, Amazon, and premium cable channels as listed in step 16.

7. One of the biggest issues you need to face immediately is that your income is probably going to be cut by half or more. Your expenses are not going to be cut by half. If

your spouse was drawing Social Security and already received the monthly payment for the month in which death occurred, you must give the money back. You can apply for a one-time death benefit from the Social Security Administration (SSA) for around $255.00. Survivor benefits may be available for children under age sixteen (or disabled children of any age). Schedule an appointment with your local SSA office so that you can confirm what your ongoing benefits will be.

Upon the death of a spouse, you are eligible for a Social Security survivor benefit if you have been married for at least nine months. (This length of marriage requirement is waived if you are caring for a child of the deceased spouse that is under the age of sixteen). If you and your spouse had both already started claiming Social Security, the higher benefit amount becomes the survivor benefit, and the lower of the two benefit amounts will be stopped. If your deceased spouse (or ex-spouse) had begun benefits but you had not, you will have some choices to make when you claim the survivor benefit. In many cases, this choice can be made in a way that is likely to give you more lifetime income. It depends on the age at which you begin benefits. You can collect a monthly benefit as early as age sixty, but at this age you will only receive about 70 percent of the amount you could get if you wait until your survivor full retirement age (which is age sixty-six for people born in 1943–1954 and gradually increases to age sixty-seven for people born in 1960 or later). Note: Full retirement age to qualify for survivor benefits uses a different date of birth table than full retirement age to qualify for your own retirement benefit. If you are disabled, you can collect a Social Security survivor's benefit as early as age fifty.

8. If the deceased served in the armed forces, there may be Veteran's Administration (VA) survivor benefits payable to the spouse and/or the children of the deceased veteran. While some benefits require that the death occurred while on active duty, others just require service. You should contact the VA to determine if you qualify. Be prepared to supply any discharge papers that are available and a copy of the death certificate.

9. Locate any life insurance policies, including ones from employment. If you are not sure whether an employer offered a life insurance benefit, call the company's human resources department and ask. Once you receive the death certificates, you should contact every insurance company where the deceased had a

policy. These may include employer-sponsored plans, individually owned policies, mortgage cancellation plans, and possibly policies issued by associations, banks, and credit cards companies. Some of these policies, especially the last three, may only provide benefits if the death resulted from an accident. Other policies may provide an additional benefit for accidental death.

When you receive the payments from insurance policies, please realize that you are not rich. This money needs to last you for as long as possible. That was the purpose in purchasing the life insurance policy. Divide the amount received by your annual household income from last year's tax return, and you can quickly determine how long the money could last you. For the time being, live as frugally as possible until you have a chance to figure out your expenses against your reduced income.

10. As a widow or widower, if you were covered by your spouse's health insurance, you may be entitled to continue your current health coverage for thirty-six months through the Consolidated Omnibus Budget Reconciliation Act (COBRA) program. If you do not have other health insurance, you can apply for COBRA through your spouse's former health plan within sixty days of when you would lose coverage or when you receive a notice for electing COBRA. You will be asked to pay the monthly premium cost. Be aware that COBRA is not a guaranteed benefit, and companies do not have to offer it or continue it. It is considered discretionary, and contrary to public opinion, it is not mandated or supervised by the federal government.

11. Notify financial institutions. You will need to notify all savings and investment companies

where the deceased had an account. This includes both individually owned accounts and joint accounts. You will have to provide a death certificate and Letters Testamentary for each account and then set up new accounts in the names of the heirs to receive the assets. You should also contact any pension providers to determine whether the pension benefit includes survivor payments.

12. Contact mortgage companies (read my next chapter on First Line of Defense) and other loan providers, including credit card companies. Because these debts are now obligations of the deceased's estate, they will have to be paid off by the assets of the estate. One exception is if the deceased was married. In that instance, the responsibility may transfer to the spouse.

13. It is also a good idea to contact the credit bureaus and report the death to prevent

identity theft after your loved one's passing. The executor should also request a copy of the deceased's credit report.

14. Figure out your net worth and a monthly budget. If you are not used to working with a monthly budget, start with your bank statements (available online) for the last three months and your check register to fill in the basic expenses. Be sure to include a monthly allowance for items that are deducted quarterly, semiannually, or annually, such as Home Owners Association (HOA) fees, termite, home warranty, and vehicle insurance.

15. If you are making vehicle payments and no longer need the vehicle, check the blue book value and determine if you are upside down on the car loan. If so, consider returning it to the dealer. Do not sign anything making you responsible for the difference between the

money owed and what they will resell the vehicle for.

16. You will have to deal with how to access and/or cancel your loved one's various online accounts and subscriptions. These include:

a. Online Banking

If an account isn't held jointly or in a trust, it won't be accessible until the deceased's estate is settled in court. A judge may issue a letter allowing the executor or estate administrator to access the account solely to pay final expenses, such as funeral costs.

If you are not a cosigner on the account, you should not attempt to forge the deceased's signature, pay bills, or sign checks in his or her name. This is fraud, as is any unauthorized access to someone's bank account.

b. Social Media

Each social media site has its own policy for handling accounts of deceased members. You will need to prove that the death has occurred and that you have been authorized to act on behalf of the deceased before you can access or delete the account. Here are the most used sites:

Facebook – In advance of death, users can either choose to memorialize the account or have it permanently deleted. Memorializing the account allows someone to share one last post from the account—in case they want to share funeral plans or post a tribute—change the profile picture and cover photo as well as respond to new friend requests. Any posts shared before the account was memorialized cannot be edited or removed.

Twitter cooperates with an authorized

point of contact to work on deactivating an account after the user dies. However, Twitter will not allow someone to have account access to post anything or make any changes to the account.

LinkedIn has a similar policy to Twitter, in that the deceased user's accounts will be closed out when requested by a friend or family member if they can provide the death certificate.

Google accounts (Google+, Gmail, YouTube, and Google search history) – If an advanced directive feature was not set up, you can close out the account or request data; however, it's up to Google's discretion to hand over data.

Yahoo! allows verified friends or family members to close out the user's account upon death. No one can request data from Yahoo! or access the deceased

73

person's account.

Pinterest, like Twitter, LinkedIn and Yahoo accounts, can only be closed out upon request by verified friends or family members.

Instagram allows friends and family to request that the deceased user's account be memorialized or deleted.

Microsoft e-mail accounts (Hotmail, Live, MSN, or Outlook) allow users to submit a Next of Kin request prior to death. This request allows users to choose what happens to the account if they die — either close it out or keep it active. Unlike *Facebook*, family and friends won't get access to the account, but *Microsoft* will send them a DVD with the account's data. Other *Microsoft* accounts like OneDrive or Skype don't have a formal policy yet regarding the issue of deceased users.

c. Cell Phone Contracts

To cancel or transfer a cell phone contract after the death of your loved one, simply call the provider's support number and tell the representative what you want to do and why. You should have the following information on hand when you call.

- Account holder's name
- Mobile phone number of the deceased
- Date of passing
- Last 4 digits of the customer's Social Security Number (SSN)
- Your name and number
- A death certificate

d. Other Accounts to Consider

Online Business – If your loved one had any online commerce accounts they probably include one or more from Amazon, PayPal, or eBay. You will need to contact these companies directly.

Online Subscriptions – These accounts can be cancelled by contacting the customer service department.

- Netflix
- Hulu Plus
- Amazon Prime
- Credit cards
- Newspapers
- Magazines
- Utilities – Internet, cable

These are the basics to get you started. If you do not already have access to an accountant, you will need one, as well as a financial advisor, depending on the scope of your assets.

Chapter Four
First Line of Defense

I recently had lunch with my mortgage banker friend to pick her brain about the immediate steps or first line of defense a homeowner should take after losing his/her spouse. The evil reality is that in a two-paycheck family your income is going to be drastically cut, sometimes by as much as 50 percent to 70 percent. My friend had some interesting advice.

1. The absolute first thing to do is to call your mortgage lender's loan service department. Their contact information is listed on your

statement or loan papers. Let them know your spouse has passed, and ask them to make notes in your file to that effect. This one notification phone call will set a whole different pace to any future action taken by the mortgage holder.

2. Assess your situation. Can you make all your payments, or do you need to make adjustments? Determine where you are financially and if you want to stay in your home. Can you take in a boarder for a short-term period? Do not advertise for a roommate on Craigslist. You are in a vulnerable position and state of mind. Network through friends, church, or work, and so forth to find a suitable referral. This has no negative repercussions to your credit rating.

3. Can you qualify for an interest-only loan? This is typically a thirty-year mortgage with interest-only payments the first ten years, and

then your payments are adjusted after ten years to cover your full principal over the next twenty-year period. This is especially appealing if you don't plan to stay in your current home for more than ten years.

4. Have a real estate agent come in and assess your property so you can find out how much equity you have in your home.

5. Try for a loan modification with your lender. Note: You must be two months delinquent before you can request a loan modification.

6. As a last resort, try for a short sale. A short sale is a sale of real estate in which the net proceeds from selling the property will fall short of the debts secured by liens against the property. This is pre-foreclosure, and you are restricted for up to seven years before you can apply for a new home loan.

7. Contact all other creditors to apprise them of your situation, including your HOA, because

the HOA can very quickly file a lien on your property if you fall behind on their payments. An HOA lien must be satisfied before you can sell your home or this can upset a short sale.

Always have someone else review your paperwork before you sign it. This should be someone not in the grief circle with you. If you don't have a savvy friend and can't afford a lawyer, try your local legal aid clinic. There are laws restricting "predatory lending," but you will occasionally run into an unscrupulous lender.

I hope you will never need this advice, but I offer it as words from the wise. Experience is a great teacher.

Chapter Five
Enjoy Your Stay in Jail

These were the final words yelled at my friend by a supposed Internal Revenue Service (IRS) agent before he hung up on her. It all started with a voicemail that a female caller left on her home phone with words to the effect of "This is Lauren Matthews from the IRS. Return this call immediately regarding the imminent seizure of your property and impoundment of all bank account funds. Do not ignore this phone call."

My friend, anxiety already starting to rise, returned the call immediately, and was told the call was being recorded, and she had an outstanding debt of $30,000 including tax, penalties, and interest. Before she could ask any questions, the agent said he had to read a statement to her outlining rights and laws she was subject to and what the "counts" were in the "lawsuit." The two pages sounded official and terrifying. She asked why she hadn't been notified of this before, and the agent said correspondence had been sent to her home address, which he recited to her as well as her e-mail address. She asked for specifics, and he said he had to transfer her to another agent for that information and to set up payment arrangements.

The next guy also said the conversation was being recorded. When she requested specific information like years of tax returns with amounts owed, dates of the letters sent, and that requested copies be sent out again, he became verbally abusive and threatened her with the sheriff coming to arrest her within hours if she didn't take care of the delinquency immediately. When she said she needed more information, he shouted "Enjoy your stay in jail," and disconnected the call. The call itself lasted about fifteen minutes.

Within minutes after the disconnection, her phone rang, and the caller said he was from a state regulatory agency, which my friend didn't recognize. He said that her driver's license had been revoked, and it was illegal for her to drive her vehicle.

My friend called me in an almost hysterical state and related this awful story about her funds being impounded, her property seized, possibly going to jail for a $30,000 debt she didn't know anything about, and that her driver's license had been suspended. I asked a few questions ascertaining she had not received any correspondence from the IRS, she had not received any driving citations, and she had not let her insurance lapse. I told her I was sure it was a scam because that's not how the IRS operates.

My friend is a well-educated, rational business woman, and a widow who happened to be going through a stressful period. She was totally unprepared for a blitz attack from some corrupt vermin who make their living by preying on unsuspecting individuals. Widows and widowers who are stressed are especially susceptible and vulnerable. This strikes at the very core of who they are because they have already lost their center, which makes them more at risk and more apt to believe someone who acts as if in authority and is abusive and threatening.

After I "talked her off the ledge," she got her panic under control and took some positive actions. She found out the police could not do anything because a crime hadn't occurred although there was an apparent attempt at extortion. She filed a report with the IRS phishing department to report the scam. She also contacted the Department of Motor

Vehicles (DMV) to confirm that her license was in good standing and there were no outstanding tickets or warrants. Additionally, she put a freeze on her credit so that no one could open any new accounts without her being notified first of the application.

I googled the phone number the supposed agent had left and found out there were numerous reports of scam phone calls from this number purporting to be calls and messages from the IRS. I also found out the IRS placed phone scams as number one on its tax scams list this year, up from number two last year, after receiving more than 90,000 complaints about such calls. To set the record straight, the IRS will never:

1. Initiate contact with you by phone. You will always be contacted by mail sent to the same address as used on your tax returns.
2. Call you asking for personal or financial information.
3. Call you and demand immediate payment

without the opportunity to appeal through the mail.

4. Call you and require that you pay your taxes over the phone through a specific method such as by credit card, debit card, or with a wire transfer.

5. Call and threaten you with arrest, audit, deportation, or suspension of your driver's license or business license.

6. Call and be angry, aggressive, emotional, abusive, or hostile.

7. Have the police, Department of Motor Vehicles (DMV), or other law enforcement groups call you and say they will come and arrest you if you don't pay.

Getting back to my friend, shouldn't it be a crime to subject someone to profound distress and anxiety with the intent to extort funds? Days later, she is still very upset over the ordeal. I don't know how soon this group of thieves will be caught and prosecuted, but I do believe that karma is a bitch, and preying on victims with fragile psyches should double that curse.

Chapter Six
Minor Changes for Major Impact

Part of me wants to tell you to just leave everything in place for the moment. Don't put your home on the market, start awfulizing major life changes, or tackling drastic decluttering projects. Unless you are in imminent danger of foreclosure or eviction, just back away and give yourself some time for things to settle. The other part of me wants you to consider replacing your bed linens, comforter, or bedspread, and your bed if you can afford to. This will give a fresh look to the bedroom and buffer the constant shock you get when you walk into a familiar space expecting to see your love. When Jerry's illness progressed to the point where he required the use of a hospital bed, he asked that it not be placed in the great room where we had plenty of space to set it up. He wanted to maintain a bit of dignity and hold onto some sense of privacy. We had the king-sized bed we shared in our master bedroom dismantled and then swapped with the trundle bed we used in our guest room. That way, I could still sleep close to him on the trundle bed while he rested on the hospital bed placed in our bedroom, which allowed him privacy. The trundle bed was already stacked with colorful cushions and became a lounge for visitors to relax on during the day as they spent time with Jerry.

The week after Jerry passed, I visited a department store and purchased a new queen-sized bed and headboard. In the linens department, I selected a quilted print comforter and shams completely different from our elegant king-sized tapestry bedspread, which required two people to handle when making the bed. The difference in the bed size and appearance was enough to jolt me into not searching for Jerry every time I entered the bedroom. And being able to make the bed up by myself helped me stop picturing the "Honey, let's make the bed," routine we shared every morning before we left the house.

In the master bathroom, I normally used the bathtub, and Jerry liked to take a shower each morning, so we had separate towel racks. He would drape his towels on the rack and over the shower door to dry. When it came to selecting towels from the linen closet, I was "matchy-match" and he was not. His rack looked so empty to me each time I entered the bathroom. I took a set of pretty guest towels that looked brand new and hung them on Jerry's towel rack in the master bathroom beside the shower. It filled the space, and because I knew he would never have chosen to hang them together, I was distracted from being reminded of him each time I entered the bathroom. Jerry normally shaved in the guest bathroom, so all his toiletries were in the guest medicine cabinet or stored in the cabinets under the sink. This was the first area I was comfortable with clearing out. I asked my stepson to take home any of the colognes and grooming products he wanted and discard the rest.

It's important to not allow anyone to start handling, sorting, or packing up your loved one's possessions without your permission or request for help. Friends and family members may offer to take over this task, thinking it will spare you effort and pain. If they need something to do, ask them to clean out the refrigerator and freezer. Trust me, this request will immediately shut them down. You need to proceed at your own pace when you have had time to contemplate how you want to distribute clothing, jewelry, and other possessions. If you are not planning on an immediate move from your home, what's the rush? Allow yourself some time to get used to being alone and to arrive at a place in your mind where you feel you can make rational decisions. Think about relatives or friends who would enjoy having some of the belongings you plan to distribute. Jerry had made up a list of small bequests for his watch collection, some pieces of art glass, and his favorite silk Tommy Bahama shirts. He sorted through his fishing gear when he felt up to it and made up several tackle boxes for friends and for his sons. He had an extensive collection of books on the history of airplanes that he requested be sent to a family friend. I was grateful to have some directives from him.

Chapter Seven
It Is What It Is

I kept looking for lessons or clues to help me move forward in life after Jerry transitioned. I was just bummed out with my life in general. Sure, I could still smell the flowers, but no one was there to plant them for me, or water them, or pick them after they bloomed. And that analogy kind of bled over into most areas of my life.

A few months before Jerry became ill, I had a nasty fall while we were on vacation. The injury topped off my previously diagnosed spinal stenosis by further compressing my spine column—giving me the equivalent space for my spinal cord of a twelve-lane expressway feeding into two lanes—according to my surgeon. Because of the fall, I went from being able to walk a few steps unassisted, and usually navigating on crutches (with partial wheelchair backup) to becoming totally wheelchair-dependent. Three orthopedic consults later, I opted for surgery, primarily to ease my unbearable pain whenever I stood up to transfer. I hoped a secondary benefit would be regaining some of my lost mobility. Jerry was diagnosed with lung cancer three weeks after my surgery.

After several weeks of physical therapy following the surgery, it became obvious that my walking was not going to be an option. I needed the power chair full-time. By some miracle, I could continue driving. And I could care for my husband for eight months before he passed. I was suddenly in charge of the driving, shopping, meal preparation, and laundry—chores Jerry usually handled.

I became grateful to be using a power wheelchair when it came time to unload and carry in groceries from our vehicle, transport a bundle of clothes to the laundry room, or take dinner on a tray balanced on my lap from the kitchen to the bedroom so that my husband and I could eat together every evening. I would not have been able to do these things if I were using crutches. I amazed both of us with my new found domestic abilities. Jerry was no longer the care giver. We had traded places.

Three years after Jerry passed, the economy tanked, and my business closed, affecting me like another death. For the first time since I was a kid and the oldest child, I was suddenly without responsibility for anybody except myself and my pets (fur kids). With my sister's blessing and promises to care for my pups and water my plants, I loaded up my minivan and headed off on a solo road trip. I drove almost 6,000 miles roundtrip from Arizona, stopping in Arkansas to visit my Mom, then heading up to Mt. Vernon, Illinois, to see another sister and her family. From there I went to Myrtle Beach, South Carolina, to reacquaint myself with the Atlantic Ocean and to see more family and friends before heading to Iowa for a rock concert. I drove home to Arizona, passing through many small towns with empty buildings and boarded up storefronts. It was comforting in a sad way to realize that our state wasn't alone in the wretched economy, and I wasn't the only one grieving a lost business.

The road trip was very liberating for me. Some days, I played my music loud, so I wouldn't have to think. I talked to Jerry a lot, often drifting away from the conversation only to pick it up hours later or even the next day. I learned the words to all the songs on my Adam Lambert, Meatloaf, Pink, Lady Gaga, and Adele CDs. I allowed myself the freedom of singing and sometimes screaming at the top of my lungs. It felt good. I howled at the moon. I think it howled back. And I cried. I cried for my losses—my husband, my business, and my retirement plan of sitting on the porch swing with Jerry and living happily ever after. I might have gone a little crazy. I talked to a lot of people. I met most of them at gas stations or diners. They were friendly, often a little shy, and they asked lots of questions about what I was doing all by myself. I would grin and tell them I didn't have to be back at the home until dark. I think seeing a woman using a wheelchair and obviously traveling alone caught them off guard.

After seven weeks, I returned to Arizona. My dogs were indifferent, and my plants were still green for the most part. I had a list of priorities, and I had set some goals. I felt the beginning of a small sense of peace. And I felt incredibly empowered. I am woman, I am physically challenged, and I am invincible—or nearly.

Chapter Eight
This Is the Soundtrack of My Life

Can you hear it? Do you know the words? Come sing along with me. Better yet, write down your own soundtrack. The lyrics from your favorite songs can be a great healer. Smile at the words or melodies that bring you joy, and cry at the parts that bring back sweet memories. Most importantly, sing your little heart out to your favorite tunes, and howl at the moon if you feel like it. It is so liberating! I'd love to hear your soundtrack.

Betts McCalla

Stage One – Becoming ♀
Bridge Over Troubled Waters
Diamonds on the Soles of Her Shoes
Girls Just Wanna Have Fun
She Works Hard for the Money
Hold On
Hard Headed Woman

Stage Two – Seeking ♂
I Want to Know What Love Is
I Love Rock N Roll
Good Golly Miss Molly
Wake up Little Susie
Sgt. Pepper's Lonely Hearts Club Band
The Jack

Stage Three – Finding ♥
Respect
Joy to the World
I've Loved You Before
Turn, Turn, Turn (To Everything There is a Season)
Unchained Melody (Officially "our" song)
Somebody to Love

Stage Four – Loving ♫
You Are My Best Friend
Don't Stop Me Now
When a Man Loves a Woman

In the Midnight Hour
Pearl Necklace
A Kiss to Build a Dream On
I'm Confessin' That I Love You
I've Had the Time of My Life
What a Wonderful World

Stage Five – Breaking ♪
You Can't Lose a Broken Heart
Live Like You were Dying
Bad Moon Rising
Stormy Weather
Life Support
Angel Down
Stay
Time for Miracles
Why Me?
I Ain't the Same
To Know Him Is to Love Him
Calling All Angels

Stage Six – Grief ↓
Nobody Knows the Trouble I've Seen
You Feel So Lonely You Could Die
Ain't No Sunshine
Hallelujah
My Hero
Wind Beneath My Wings

Betts McCalla

Stage Seven – Healing ☼
Kickstart My Heart
We Are Family
If I Ruled the World
Because of You
I Can See Clearly Now
Taking Care of Business

Chapter Nine
Call Me Anytime

This chapter is for anyone who wants to help someone suffering the loss of a loved one.

"Call me if you need anything."

"Call me if I can help."

"Promise you will call and let me know how you're doing."

How many times have you uttered those thoughtful yet totally useless comments to friends or family members, who stare at you with teary eyes, looking a little shell-shocked by a recent death?

Think about it. Has anyone ever responded to

your comment? Have they mustered the humiliation and shame of admitting they had no one else to rely on so they called you, hopeful that you really meant you were available to help?

When my husband passed, everyone made those well-intentioned and empty-handed offers of help—the neighbors, the couples we considered best friends, and my girlfriends who sat with me during his surgeries and spent hours with us at hospice.

Within a few days, everyone went back to their regular lives. My regular life was gone. It had burst, broken, shattered, and lay in shambles.

No one besides my sister, Clo, said "I will call you tomorrow to see what you need." If they had called, I would have told them I needed someone to come over and sit and drink a cup of tea with me. I might have said I needed a couple of cans of soup and a loaf of bread from the grocery store or a bag of dog food because I couldn't find the energy to get in the car and drive to the store. I could have mentioned that I needed someone to empty all the food out of the refrigerator that had been stored too long and then to pull the trash can out to the curb for tomorrow's pickup. I could have told him or her that I needed a big tight hug—not the wimpy "so sorry for your loss, dearie" half-shoulder pats. How I longed for someone to take the time to just sit with me and hold my hand.

If any of us have a friend suffering from sudden onset grief, it helps to remember that he or she will feel tired, numb, and often experience brain fog. And that friend might be a little touchy. Just accept that this is the new norm for the moment, and don't make a big issue out of it. If you are in the neighborhood or can spare an hour to visit, call and say so. A short, unscheduled visit can do wonders to lift your friend's spirits. Don't expect your grieving friend to want to go to a movie, check out the local sales, or even go out to dinner anytime soon. Anything that involves more than a shower and letting his or her hair dry naturally is too much effort. If a regular cleaning service isn't evident, ask if you can vacuum the floor. If there are dishes in the sink, you might offer to unload or load the dishwasher. Small household chores are insurmountable in the face of grief. It's easy to lose track of time when you're grieving, and what seems a whole day of possibilities, dwindles away with little accomplished.

If your friend mentions a repair or some maintenance job that needs to be attended to and you know somebody that can do the job, say, "I've got a person for that" and share the contact information. My friends and I share our lists. I've always had a list because my honey was not mechanical. I learned early on in our relationship that it was simpler to just call someone and get the repair done properly.

Bring over a small bouquet or even a single bloom. For the first year, my sister bought a bouquet of roses each week from the grocery store. Roses were Jerry's favorite flowers, and it felt right and special to sit admiring them and enjoying their fragrance. Bring a box of tea or a packet of special coffee and stay long enough to brew it and share a pot. But most of all, bring your funny stories and touching memories, and say our loved one's name. Say it again and again, lest we think he or she is forgotten.

Chapter Ten
Twelve Myths About Grief

1. *Grief has a timeline or schedule.* Prior experience has taught us that a bad breakup takes about six months to get over. So we tend to think, okay, it will probably take a year to get over a death. Wrong answer. It takes however long it takes. Some people can finish their grieving process in a year. Some people might need five years or ten years or forever. You don't get over a loss. You get through it.

2. *Grief is best gone through alone.* You might

feel like being alone in the beginning, but don't perpetuate this desire to shut yourself off from people. You need people around who will say your loved one's name, talk with you about your loss, and listen as you recite memories, anecdotes, and ask universal questions that have no defined answers. Make it a point in the beginning to seldom eat dinner alone. Call a day in advance and tell your friends you'd like to dine with them tomorrow.

3. *Because you feel crazy, you are going crazy.* You are not going crazy. You are reacting to an awful thing that happened. It's natural to feel crashing waves of emotions. Try not to commit any bodily acts of harm to yourself or others during this period. Resist the temptation to take scissors to your hair.

4. *Being upset and grieving means you don't trust or believe in God and your religion.*

You can certainly question God's plan and
your place in it without losing faith. This plan
was most likely set into action before you
were born. God can handle all the rantings
and the tears you direct at Him. He loves you
unconditionally.

5. *Losing someone suddenly without warning
   has the same impact as losing someone to an
   anticipated death.* A sudden loss is intensely
   painful because it is not only shocking and
   heartbreaking—there is a devastating and
   unsettling lack of closure. Losing someone
   suddenly means not having the opportunity to
   say "Goodbye" and "I'll love you forever."
   On the other hand, saying goodbye repeatedly
   as you watch your loved one die a little bit
   each day is pure agony. You wake up each
   morning wondering if this is the last day you
   will have your love alive and with you. Will
   this day be the day of your final goodbye

kiss? The bottom line is that any loss of a loved one is deeply painful whether the death is unexpected or anticipated.

6. *It will be easier if you avoid discussing the death or mentioning your loved one's name.* By not speaking about your loss and saying and hearing his or her name, you delay the grieving process. Sometimes people think it's kinder not to mention your loved one's name, but they are withholding the healing you need.

7. *Grief support groups are depressing and maudlin.* Not all supports groups will be the right fit for you. Give several a try until you find a group you are comfortable with. You can join a grief support group at any stage of your grief even if it's a year or two after your loss. If you don't want to expose your feelings to a group, seek out a therapist or counselor to work with on an individual basis.

8. *Grief must be handled in stages.* Grief may come in stages, but the stages (shock or disbelief, denial, anger, bargaining, guilt, depression, acceptance, and hope) won't be in any particular order. And there's no rule that one, two, or three stages can't all show up at once, making a triple whammy. Take it a day at a time, and if that seems too hard, back it down to an hour at a time. Remember to breathe.

9. *Tears are a sign of weakness.* Tears are a sign of healing. And they help rid your body of toxins. It's natural to start weeping at the most inopportune times following your loss. Know in advance that your eyes are going to well up several times a day when you least expect it. Give up wearing eye makeup for a while.

10. *We only grieve deaths.* Impactful losses of any kind need to be grieved. They can be the

loss of a marriage, a business, a home, or a country. Any loss that wrenches at your core deserves proper grieving so that you can move past it.

11. *Time heals all wounds.* Time eases pain. That heart-wrenching, unbearable pain felt during early grief will eventually become more bearable. But, because love never dies, time itself can't fix the brokenness and emptiness you feel—that can only come from inner courage, peace, and love. No matter how much time passes, holidays and special occasions without your loved one will always feel a little empty. Random things that you associate with that person will continue to trigger your memory; however, time can unfortunately fade or steal a piece of that memory. All of that is normal. There is no time schedule as to how long grief will last. So, no, time does not heal all wounds.

12. *I will never be happy again.* If you were once happy, you can be happy again. But it will be different because your life and your circumstances have changed. You might not be as accepting of your friends' idiosyncrasies, and you may decide some activities are too shallow to indulge in. Look for small pleasures in everyday activities so that you retain some semblance of your prior lifestyle. You might even notice that colors appear to have a different hue and brightness, but they are still beautiful in the new shades. Familiar foods may possibly taste different or seem tasteless. Experiment until you find something sustaining. Eat protein every day, and make a conscious effort to stay healthy. If going to the gym doesn't appeal to you right now, consider venturing outside for a short walk at the beach or park or just sitting in your own flower garden—wherever you feel

at peace. Maybe grab a green tea latte—the matcha in the tea will relax you, and a bit of sunshine and fresh air will do you a world of good.

Chapter Eleven
When You Don't Know How to Say Goodbye

I recently had dinner with a dear friend visiting from Montana where she's lived for the past fifteen years. When Jerry and I moved to California back in the late seventies, Katherine was one of the first friends we made, and she stuck. She introduced us to wonderful things that were available in California like the Sherman Library and Gardens in Corona Del Mar and the Norton Simon Museum in Pasadena. She encouraged us to camp at beautiful Big Sur and took us to our first dude ranch in Three Rivers. She even explained that those funny bumps on the freeways that alert you if you stray out of your lane were called "Botts dots," named for the man who invented them, Elbert D. Botts, a California Department of Transportation (Caltrans) engineer.

When plan A doesn't work out for her, she always has a plan B. I admire her greatly. Jerry loved to cook, and years ago Katherine started a catering company. They were often found in the kitchen together possibly plotting out the perfect recipe for meatballs in dill sauce, debating the number of layers a perfect brioche for beef Wellington should have, or taste-testing an Italian wedding cake. Katherine told me early on in our friendship that she was first in line for Jerry if he ever became available. And she reiterated it on a regular basis.

When Jerry was in hospice shortly before he passed, Katherine called to check in and asked if it was possible to speak to Jerry. She said she had something very important that she wanted to tell him. He wasn't very lucid or responsive that day, but I put the phone on speaker and placed it near him so she could talk to him. She told Jerry that her life was so much richer because he had been a part of it, and she couldn't imagine not having had the experience of their friendship. This was the sweetest goodbye I've ever heard, and I've never forgotten how loved it made us feel. Maybe when you don't know how to say goodbye, you might consider saying something like this to your loved one.

Chapter Twelve
No Regrets

Is it more painful to lose someone quickly with a traumatic and shocking here-today, gone-tomorrow passing or to lose someone suffering a devastating terminal illness with expiration date unknown? I hold this discussion in my head frequently. Three years before Jerry was diagnosed with stage 4 lung cancer, he almost died from complications of bypass surgery following a heart attack. As I mentioned earlier, during surgery both lungs collapsed, and he was on a vent for nineteen days in a medically induced coma during which he contracted a MRSA infection. Several times, prayers were answered, and he remained viable.

After a six-month recovery period, we started on bonus years. I didn't know to call them bonus years at the time. That's a term I learned later from a hospice nurse. I just knew we were blessed that he was still alive. We converted to a healthier food plan. We started the "chicken years." Beef and bacon became memories of bygone taste experiences. Cheese was no longer a snack food. Cheese and crackers were not to be considered a meal. Butter was rationed, and whole-wheat bread became the staple rather than a choice. Fruit took up more space in our refrigerator, and fresh seasonal vegetables covered our kitchen counters. Ice cream desserts were replaced by nonfat (tasteless) frozen yogurt or sherbet. The can opener was only used to open dog or cat food. We spent more time on food gathering and preparation. We talked a lot about mortality, second chances, and what we considered

God's loud wake-up call.

Jerry strictly adhered to the cardio-exercise program. Medications and follow-up doctors' appointments were meticulously scheduled. And we had three, albeit structured, years to appraise our lives, entertain friends, embrace family, and generally live well. We took long weekend vacations and cut back on work hours. We thought we were home free. We talked a bit about retiring, and what we would be doing when we had more leisure time to spend together. We daydreamed some wonderful fishing adventures (I would be doing retail therapy instead because I get seasick) in New Zealand, Costa Rica, and other exotic locales. We made bucket lists of places and friends to visit.

And then a routine chest X-ray showed a malignant mass. Surgery, chemo, radiation, bone fractures, horrible bouts of pain, hospitalizations, and hospice quickly followed. Within eight months, Jer Bear was gone. But during that period, we had

127

time to talk, to decide on his bequests, and to invite friends and family to visit. So, which is less painful: sudden or anticipated loss? I honestly don't know, but I do know that having that time, difficult as it was, gave us the opportunity to reassure each other that in our relationship we had "no regrets."

Chapter Thirteen
Wishin' and Hopin'

When you are grieving, it takes a tremendous amount of energy to get from point A (we'll call it your bed)—to point B (we'll call it taking in nourishment by locating the kitchen)—to point C (cleaning up, putting on street clothes, and leaving the house). If you are not required to show up at a 9-to-5 position, it is very easy for the days to run together. Do you ever realize as you are sitting at your computer reading e-mails or checking Facebook for the umpteenth time, you are not sure what day it is? Is it Friday or Saturday? You experience a slight rise of panic as you hurriedly check the date at the bottom of your computer screen or grapple for your cell phone or a calendar hidden under the stack of loose papers on your desk. Lacking structure for each day causes a maelstrom of hours lost to inactivity, lethargy, and indifference. You wish you could turn back time to those few hours before you fell off the earth—back to just before the tipping point of no return when your loss became irrevocable.

When I was a young child, I would seize the annual Sears Christmas catalog known as the *wish book*. I would spend countless hours as I pored over the pages, carefully making my choices of gifts for each member of my family and, of course, for myself. I would take sheets of notepaper and copiously list a brief description of each coveted item along with the page number and the price—a very rudimentary example of those Excel spreadsheets we later learned to endure. Little did I know I was setting myself up for my current wish list exercise known as Amazon Prime. I find when I am being held telephone-captive, especially waiting on hold to reach a live customer service person like at an insurance company, cable company, or a government agency, I idly peruse the world's largest online wish book, seeking that same vicarious childhood thrill of the hunt and discovery. I make various wish lists and then flood them with items I have no intent or the means to purchase.

Wishing (less than 5 percent fulfillment possibility): Feel or express a strong desire for something that is not easily attainable; want something that cannot or probably will not happen.

Hoping (95 percent fulfillment possibility): To desire, especially with expectation that the wish will be granted.

Until my husband passed, I never realized there was a big difference between those two words. I just thought it was a cute song, sung by Dusty

Springfield. You know the one I mean? *Wishin' and hopin' and thinkin' and prayin'...*

Hoping is to desire something with a full expectation that the wish will be granted. This expectation is usually fueled by actions on your part to ensure it happens. For instance, hoping to get a good job would mean preparation by taking classes, training, and finally submitting a kick-ass resume and killer cover letter to a range of prospective employers. Hoping to meet someone special would entail researching the qualities you desire and then showing up, appropriately attired, at a venue where the type of person you want to meet would most likely frequent. These points of contact could be universities, museums, churches, concerts, sporting events, or food emporiums. I have firsthand knowledge of successful meetings at each of the locations with the addition of a laundromat (think Irish troubadour band imported for St. Paddy's Day in Chicago).

Wishing, on the other hand, would be reading the job ads and daydreaming of spending the proposed salary on purchases, lifestyle changes, and vacation trips, but never taking classes or spending time training to learn and hone the required skills to make yourself qualified for the position you are seeking. Another example is wishing to meet someone special, and then spending time searching profiles online without putting yourself on the line.

Bottom line: Hope is possible if you are willing to do the work. Wishing steals valuable time that you could be using to fulfill your hopes. It's your choice.

Chapter Fourteen
Set Peace of Mind as Your Highest Goal

Peace of mind, to me, is the absence of mental stress or anxiety. I attempt to achieve this by calming down my brain each day by systematically eliminating as many of the unnecessary, busy thoughts as I can from my head. First thing in the morning, I turn on the coffee machine and open the window blinds, so I can check that the world is still out there and intact. I give some quality ear-scratching time to the fur kids and wash and refill their water and food dishes.

Then, I take about fifteen minutes to clear my

head of negative thoughts by placing them in a visualized, tightly covered, waste bin that I've labeled "Toxic Trash." This is not your friendly recyclable bin. Some days, I must stop mid-practice and make a list of grocery items I need to purchase as thoughts of tomatoes, green peppers, bags of lettuce, cookies, and containers of milk won't quit ricocheting around until I list them on paper. Often memories of stressful confrontations or thoughtless comments people have made, which are still waiting for my snarky comeback, swoosh in unbidden, causing disruptions in my quietude. I quickly stuff them into the trash can and move on. Some days, I can't stop spinning problems or replaying conversations. Then I feel out of sorts all day because I didn't achieve peace of mind. Maybe I need a bigger trash can. But some days, like today, the world feels right, and I'm grateful for my place in it. Oh, and thank God, the coffee is ready.

"Set peace of mind as your highest goal, and organize your life around it."

– Brian Tracy

Chapter Fifteen
Identity Fraud

We associate this term most often with credit card theft and data breaches of which there have been many in the news lately. But what about the people we know? How many are walking around using identity fraud? I don't mean stolen identities for credit gain. I'm talking about the many identities we paste on for our day-to-day going-through-the-motions activities. The fast "I'm in a hurry, no time to talk" persona we use at the grocery store, as we race our carts toward the checkout finish line. The earbuds worn connected to our cell phones indicate we are in a state of listening to something of immense importance, so don't you dare interrupt us to ask a question, directions, or so forth, as we stand in line to purchase our lattes. We insulate ourselves from public contact. We drive directly into our garages, closing the door before exiting our vehicle. We work in our yards surrounded by seven-foot-high fences. When approached by a stranger in a public place, we tend to view him or her as a possible threat rather than as someone making a friendly overture. At what point did we become so fearful and adopt those behaviors?

Some of us used to have yet another identity when we were half of a whole couple. When we had a couple name like BettsandJerry. I felt braver then because I knew someone always had my back or was there to offer me a hand up. I had a full-time cheerleader, a live-in fashion consultant, and someone who loved me unconditionally. I knew someone was expecting me home and would send out the gendarmes if I didn't show up. If I was sick, I didn't need to arrange for a ride to the doctor or the emergency room. I never had to eat a meal alone unless by choice. I had an entertaining travel companion who shared the driving and was always up for a road trip. And then life changed, and I became half, desperately missing my other half. I learned to make concessions. I had to step up my game. If I wanted a road trip, then I went on a road trip, doing the driving myself. I tried on all the above-mentioned "avoid and elude the public" identities, but these actions just served to isolate me more.

Gradually, I began to rebuild myself into a new whole. I had a security system installed, and when I moved to a new home, I made friendly overtures to my neighbors and joined the neighbor block watch. During a recent local power outage, my neighbors on both sides called to make sure I was okay. Those calls made me feel cared about.

I've learned the names of all the dogs I encounter walking with their people on the way to my mailbox. I do still refer to the owners as Skippy's mom or Molly's dad. And, I've even started talking to strangers in the produce department at my local grocery store. I ask them questions like "How would you cook this?" while holding up an eggplant or something yellow and orange with bumps. They often look a little fearful as I approach them, but I can usually elicit a smile or two and sometimes a good cooking tip.

Chapter Sixteen
It's the Little Things

How was your day? The most common, innocuous question everyone asks is also the one most missed when you arrive home and no one is there to ask. The freedom to walk in the door, go to your partner for an embrace and murmur, "Enh," as your response, knowing full well he or she will understand and be willing to listen to all the gory details. Or those days you say, "Good," with enthusiasm, your partner's eyes light up with interest waiting to share a triumph. With either answer, you have someone's attention. Someone cares how the world treated you today, and if you got shat upon, your partner will put it all into perspective. If kudos are in order, he or she will break out the champagne. But the important thing is someone was there to ask.

I miss the small gestures in a relationship. The caress on the shoulder or the hip bump as you perform a small *pas de deux* preparing a meal together. The steadying hand at your elbow as you traverse steps or a rocky incline. The intertwining of fingers that have always seemed to fit together. The confidence and assurance derived from knowing that there is a person in your world who accepts you unconditionally and always has your back. These things make up the day-to-day gist of a loving relationship. You feel brave, protected, and competent. When that reflection is no longer available, your hackles rise, you are fearful, lonely, and feel clumsily out of step with the rest of your world.

If you are lucky, friends, pets, and family members intervene to smooth out your edges. This smoothing process takes time because they don't know how to make you feel happy, peaceful, calm, and loved. But if you are very lucky, they won't give up, and someday you will again say you feel confident, strong, and capable. And you will be.

Chapter Seventeen
Six Stupid Things People Said to Me

1. At least you know where he is.

Excuse me, I always knew where he was. We always checked in with each other throughout the day.

2. You'll just need one car now.

Hmmm. Do you want to buy the other one? Make me an offer.

3. It'll be easier to cook for one person.

That might be true, if you were the one doing the cooking. I lost my cook, too, in addition to my best friend, companion, cheerleader, and lover. Dinner quickly became a large cup of coffee and a big cookie, or a bag of popcorn. An ice cream cone made a well-balanced meal. It covered all the food groups when you got it with fruit and nuts.

4. *Your expenses will be less now.*

But not half, like my income. This is a scary something no one talks to you about.

5. *One weird comment* came from my oral surgeon. He said that he had heard women were happiest on the day they married their husbands and on the day they buried their husbands, and was that true in my case? This came from a man who had also treated Jerry as his patient and had seen us together. I located a new oral surgeon the next time I needed one.

And my favorite... drum roll, please.

6. *We need a new death certificate.* Me: What happened to the one I gave you?

It expired. They expire after 3 months. Me: Oh, my gosh, is he coming back? No one told me that happens. I'm so excited! *Click*—that was the sound of the mortgage banker representative hanging up on me.

Chapter Eighteen

Say My Name, Say My Name

Often when a spouse or partner passes, loneliness sneaks in very quietly on padded feet. You think you are doing fine, and you suddenly realize you have not left the house or spoken to a human for several days or longer. You need to reach out and have someone say your name, to acknowledge you, and to confirm you are still viable, still visible.

Recently, a friend posted an article on Facebook about a program in England called *The Silver Line Helpline*, a twenty-four-hour call center for older adults seeking to fill a basic need: contact with other people. Often people withdraw without being noticed and will go days and sometimes weeks without any interpersonal contact. This is particularly true in instances where there are no relatives living close by, and the individual's social circumstances have changed due to loss of a spouse or siblings or possibly relocation of grown children to other parts of the country.

According to the article, researchers have found mounting evidence linking loneliness to physical illness and to functional and cognitive decline. As a predictor of early death, loneliness eclipses obesity. Recent research has shown that loneliness affects several key bodily functions, at least in part through over stimulation of the body's stress response. Chronic loneliness is associated with increased levels of a major stress hormone called cortisol as well as higher vascular resistance, which can raise blood pressure and decrease blood flow to vital organs.

If you or someone you know is caught in this loneliness trap, establish a quick phone call habit every day or two. A short phone chat consisting of even a minute or two just to say "Hi," and ask "How are you feeling today?" helps break the isolation barrier. Encourage scheduling continuous weekly activities like attending church service, going to the library, or to the grocery store. And remember to "say my name, say my name."

"When you love someone, you say their name different. Like it's safe inside your mouth." — Jodi Picoult, *Handle With Care*

Chapter Nineteen
Friday Night At a Séance

On a recent Friday night, I attended a group séance hosted by well-regarded local medium, Susanne Wilson. It's important to understand that all mediums are psychics but not all psychics are mediums. Susanne started the meeting by sharing some basic information about the possible visitors that might contact us through her. She said not to concentrate on someone showing up. I had attended a couple of large groups like this before and hadn't had any contact from loved ones that had passed on. This time I got lucky. After several messages to other people in the audience, Susanne described a man appearing to her and gave his initials. She said he's turned around and telling a story to the people behind him. They are laughing and saying they already heard that one. Susanne said he's a character. He tells funny stories, is strong, gregarious, and has a great personality. She said when he was here, he had many friends—had never met a stranger. Many people loved him, and he was a man of his word who loved taking care of his family. I claimed him.

Then his thoughts started coming through. He talked about his seventieth birthday and what a nice birthday party we gave him. Jerry died when he was sixty-nine. On his seventieth birthday, some close friends and family met in Sedona, Arizona, for a Celebration of Life party. We had a wonderful lunch, visiting with each other at Jerry's favorite local restaurant, The Hideaway. After lunch, we caravanned to Banjo Bill Picnic Site in Oak Creek

Canyon where we used to camp overnight or just spend the day. Jerry's best friend, Ed, a Christian minister, said a few words and a prayer. We shared some stories and sang "Happy Birthday to You." Then our oldest son, Brian, climbed down to the creek and spread Jerry's ashes just above his favorite fishing hole. It was a perfect day.

Susanne received several messages from Jerry for me. They were all on target, very positive, loving thoughts. I felt they were coming directly from my husband, as they were apropos to our life. He said he likes it when I talk out loud to him—usually when I'm driving. He said he will give messages and opinions, and he wants to discuss politics with me. (Apparently, everyone does these days.) He also mentioned the anniversary of his death two days before and revealed quite a bit more. I think I had the longest, most complete session. I ended the evening elated by his visit, high from the wonderful energy of the people in the room, and eager to hear from him again.

I recently upgraded my smartphone and planned to give my existing phone to my mom. I had the settings folder open to change a few things over for her use, when all of a sudden, the phone started flashing with what looked like a bright pink strobe light. If I moved my hand away, it stopped, but if I moved it back over the face of the phone, it started flashing again. This went on for several seconds, as I continued to move my hand back and forth. Amazed, I showed the phone to my mom. She said, "That phone is always acting up. It never even shows the weather right." Well, I'm pretty sure it was a bling hello from my guy.

Chapter Twenty
Tarred and Feathered

"... And you do come out of it, that's true. After a year, after five. But you don't come out of it like a train coming out of a tunnel, bursting through the downs into sunshine and that swift, rattling descent to the Channel; you come out of it as a gull comes out of an oil-slick. You are tarred and feathered for life."

— Julian Barnes, Flaubert's Parrot

Tarred and feathered for life appeals to me as an apt description of grief. Today, I was trying to come up with one word that describes my ongoing emotional state. The word I keep coming back to is "fear." I feel fearful. There is that constant annoying little scary edge to everything that shouts, "Danger, Danger." Sometimes it whispers in more of an indoor voice, "danger, danger," lulling me in before suddenly throwing the equivalent of a bucket of ice water over my head like the ALS (Amyotrophic Lateral Sclerosis or Lou Gehrig's Disease) challenges that were so popular. You know what's going to happen and you steel yourself for it, but it totally whacks you when the grief rises up in waves and takes over.

Having recently moved, I was unpacking a box of office minutiae, and in the bottom of the box was a beautiful valentine card that I had saved from Jerry. As I opened the card, I knew exactly how his signature would read. "All my love, Jer Bear" was written in his large distinctive script. Yes, the waves hit, and I felt my heart being squeezed. And then I realized I am fearful that a time will come when I won't feel the waves.

Chapter Twenty-One
Don't Be Afraid to Make a Change

I'm not sure what I should choose to worry about today. Is an earthquake imminent in California because of the reports of excess carbon monoxide readings? Was the scientific measuring equipment really faulty? Or is that report a subterfuge one political party is foisting onto the other?

For years, my husband and I were news junkies, always striving to stay up to date on every newsworthy story, often following developing news stories as though we had a personal investment in the outcome. We ate breakfast with Good Morning

America, and if we were home for dinner, we prepared our meals while watching the evening news, and then we went to bed with the nightly news. After Jerry passed, I realized watching the news alone made me feel kind of like "too-much-coffee" anxious. It was hard to deal with the constant negativity, murders, reports of road rage, corruption in government, and war fatalities.

I decided to take a time-out from all that angst, so I gave myself permission to not pay attention. And basically, nothing bad happened from my news avoidance. My insurance rates didn't increase or decrease, my hair didn't fall out or become thicker, and my weight stayed the same. Instead of watching up-to-the-minute reporting, reading daily newspapers, weekly news magazines, and loading up my DVR with sensationalized news programs that I dreaded but felt obligated to watch, I record one news program a week, CBS Sunday Morning. I find my friends and family keep me up to date on what's relevant. It's much nicer to get their news over lunch or via a Facebook message, Twitter, or Instagram.

Chapter Twenty-Two
My "Third Act"

Sometimes I feel I am on life's longest running scavenger hunt. A scavenger hunt is distinguished from a treasure hunt, in that the latter involves one or a few items that are desirable and completed in sequence, while a scavenger hunt primarily collects undesirable or useless objects in random order. And my lists seem to be cross-matched. The kitchen hunt-think trip to the grocery store midway through my list suddenly becomes an all-out effort to gather requested items for the food bank we support at church by bringing donations the first Sunday of each month. My time expands into the nature hunt that involves some judicial weeding in the backyard. I find those scissors, now rusted, that I used to trim some rosemary last month when I couldn't find the garden snippers. The post office run garners three different size priority mail boxes because I'm not sure how much room some shirts I'm planning to send my brother will take up. I stop off for a bookstore respite and a latte in their cafe. Oh look, they have a 75-percent-off table with Harry and David popcorn. I purchase four containers for the price of one. I can use them as hostess gifts to take to someone's home. What are the chances I will need four gifts before the expiration date? The question at the end of the day though, is not where you store the objects but where you store all the feelings these hunts inspire.

If life is like a play (make mine a musical) and divided into three acts, I guess I'm now in the third act. I just didn't know my "third act" would be a solo performance. My life plan included two center-row orchestra seats, and now I'm using one. I'm rewriting the script for a single front-row-seat life. I'm now solely in charge of all my life's scavenger and treasure hunts and lists. Today, I had the opportunity to hear Michelle Obama speak at a rally in downtown Phoenix. I'm learning to let my inner fan girl overcome my dislike of crowds. Tomorrow, I have my liturgical dance rehearsal (or as my sister calls it, lethargic dance). It's a praise dance group I was recently invited to join, and I only hope that my white outfit looks more angelic and less Pillsbury dough girl than I suspect. I might be the kid at the end of the row who's facing the wrong way when the music stops, but I will be participating. On Sunday, I'm attending a matinee performance of The Glass Menagerie. I splurge on season tickets at a neighborhood theater with two friends.

These are all activities that reinforce the fact

that I'm alive in this dimension. And as appreciation for the way of life I once had, I celebrate the one I now have. So, I get up, put on my good jewelry, and show up with my scavenger lists in hand.

Chapter Twenty-Three
I'd Like to Know

It's 3:00 a.m., and I'm wide awake. I turn on the dishwasher, set up the coffee pot for the morning brew, and stock the refrigerator with bottles of water and cans of diet soda. The dogs have each enjoyed their bedtime treat, and they have taken their nighttime posts, one guarding the doorway to my office and one strategically flanking the hallway. No intruders will get past these vicious ten-pound guard dogs tonight.

What I would really like at this moment is my husband to talk to. I'd like to conspiratorially trash the political candidates with someone intelligent enough to counter my arguments without lowering himself to uttering hyperbole banalities.

I'd like an opinion on whether I should have a carpenter enlarge the doorway to my bathroom or whether I should get a narrower wheelchair, which won't be as comfortable but will have a tighter turning radius. This also will cut down on the nicks and gouges to the woodwork. Or maybe I should do both?

I'd like to know whether going for physical therapy on my shoulder will be worth the time investment over the next 4 weeks or if I should just keep icing it at home.

I'd like to know whether you eat food in heaven or if you don't need it and just remain trim.

I'd like to know if you can see me missing you.

Chapter Twenty-Four
We All Still Need Recess

Free time, spare time, leisure time, time off, time-out, and recess are all units of open time—credits you have saved for yourself. Be selfish. Use them for things that make you happy. Don't squander them on chores, on overtime work, or workouts. Take a walk on the wild side, and bring your dog, a Frisbee, and a water container to a new park. Or just amble along on a leisurely stroll through a marketplace you've always thought about stopping to check out. Grab a coffee or an iced tea and sit outside on a wall or bench and people-watch for a while. Allow yourself to be calm, and reflect on the people passing by. Do they return your smile with one of their own? Do they look scared, annoyed, or friendly? What vibe are you giving off? Do you seem approachable?

Visit a nature center or a petting zoo. Allow yourself to slow down and achieve a cadence of relaxation. For the time being, just use your free-time credits for yourself. Get away from your computer, your tablet, and even turn down the ringer on your cell phone. Yes, you can afford to be out of touch for a few minutes or even an hour or two every day. Because this is your recharge time. Time to reflect on the good things in your life. Things that bring you satisfaction and joy. No guilt thoughts and no anger. Those are for another time.

We tend to schedule ourselves into a frenzy day after day. And when we finally take a break, we look around and count all the things we still plan (not need) to accomplish. Challenge yourself to schedule free time. Write it down on your calendar or enter it into your phone organizer. Set an alarm, and if you must, set a timer for when time is up. This is not TV time or Facebook time. It could be an energetic fifteen minutes of dancing to your favorite music time. Or it could even be a daytime nap.

Make it into a routine, a respite, or challenge yourself to do something different every day. Stop at the library, and take home a movie you've heard about and always meant to watch—something not available on your premium channels. Watch kids at a skateboard park or playing soccer. Try to remember when you felt that free, that brave, and that invincible. And use that smart phone to take a picture of something weird or beautiful that will remind you of how you spent your credits today.

Chapter Twenty-Five
We're Just Having an Adventure...

These were the words my husband would say to me when we were lost, and he was being too manly to stop and ask for directions. I almost starved to death one day when we were first dating because he knew the restaurant he wanted to take me to for lunch (we skipped breakfast because lunch was going to be wonderful) was just up the road about twenty miles from Mankato, and it had white pillars out front. About 3:00 p.m., he finally admitted defeat, and we settled for greasy burgers and French fries with brown gravy at a biker bar. We were having an adventure. This was in the olden days before cars came equipped with a Global Positioning System (GPS) and before all cell phones were born again as smart phones. Can you believe we drove coast to coast unaided by online directions? What pioneers we were. It was just us and those handy little TripTiks that the American Automobile Association (AAA) printed up for the asking, as part of their member services. Staying in touch with the office meant one daily phone call.

It's hard to believe how unfettered we were— and how fearless. Leaving the house now without a cell phone is tantamount to disaster. You have an improperly clothed feeling, and all day long you are reaching for your phone. These days my entire life is in my cell phone. Medical, business, and personal information all fit into the palm of my hand. It even tells me how many hours and the quality of my sleep time. The contact listing section includes past and present important and no longer important people that have been grandfathered in from my last three Android phones. I no longer bother using my battery-devouring digital Canon camera, opting instead for the convenience and acceptable quality of photos taken with my Edge.

I leave my Nook at home, as I have all the digital reading and musical apps on my phone. And my phone is faster for Internet searches than my higher priced personal computer. Just remember to edit if you use voice commands to send text messages.

Recently a friend texted her husband with "The plumber can come at six tonight. Is that OK?"

Her husband's reply (he uses voice command) was "Sex tonight is fine. Get it over with."

These electronic devices are all part of our New Now. They are adaptations we rely upon to avoid the fear of seeming vulnerable or becoming a victim. When you are alone, your sense of loneliness can breed an avoidance of intimacy. I think our lives have become so techno-dependent because we choose to avoid personal interaction with people. I wouldn't mind "having an adventure" right about now.

Chapter Twenty-Six
Practice Saying Yes

I started off last year with a resolution to say *Yes* more than *No* to invitations offering new experiences and challenges. Sometimes you can do things that are totally out of character for you just because someone asked. And without a lot of consequential hemming and hawing you said, *Yes*. Months ago, I noticed a blurb in our church bulletin mentioning that one of our members was starting a praise dance troupe and inviting people to join. I love many genres of music, am happy watching any form of creative dance, and especially enjoy praise dance as it is a joyous offering for the Lord and not a competition. I wished the dance leader luck, but it didn't mean anything special to me because let's face it, I'm in a power wheelchair.

An exchange of pleasantries with the dance leader one Sunday morning led to her spontaneous invitation for me to come and see if I would be interested in participating. For weeks at practice, I felt like the kindergartener who is always turning the wrong way and waving to parents in the audience. But it felt good to be part of this group of lovely and vital women. And seeing that I had joined, in turn encouraged another woman using a wheelchair to also join our troupe, so we had a matched set so to speak.

The applause we received at the end of our debut performance was spontaneous and heartfelt, and the positive comments reaffirmed my decision. Hearing that the wheelchairs performers added a new visual dimension made my day, and I hope our participation inspires other mobility-challenged dancers.

Don't decide that something isn't for you because you've never done it before. When you are grieving, it's easy to shut down and avoid participation in anything not necessary for day-to-day survival. I believe your loved ones who have passed are still proud of you and want you to succeed by moving forward with your life. Practice saying *Yes*. Twirl with the best of them—and at the end of the day—know you gave it a shot. You stepped out of your comfort zone and took a risk. Remember, your delivery doesn't have to be perfect, it just needs to be accomplished.

Chapter Twenty-Seven
Who Would You Be
If You Weren't Who You Are?

Does that sound like the beginning of a Dr. Seuss story or maybe a Shel Silverstein poem? But, seriously think about the different choices you made during your lifetime at each crucial bump in the road. Each bump steered you in a different direction or possibly bounced you back the way you had come—forcing you to redo a part of your life's path. I attribute one small business trip and a chance meeting with a friend of a friend to changing my life forever. The tiny ripples set off by the vibrations of that meeting affected the lives of several people and made life changes that are still being felt today. I think each person has a soul mate, and that person is born with an instinct like a homing pigeon to find you and vice versa.

From the time I was a young child, I knew I had a soul mate who was searching for me. And I was searching for him. When we finally met in a chance one-hour window of possible contact, in a city and state I was visiting for the first time, it didn't occur to me that this was my soul mate. I felt like I had met an old friend—someone I had known a long time ago. Although how could that be? There was an instant connection, a rapport, and somehow a knowingness of his character. And I remember perceiving he had an orange aura. We became best friends, business partners, lovers, spouses, and keepers of each other's heart.

There were many bumps in our road together, signaling changes in direction, in life goals, and in opportunities. There were climate changes, career

186

changes, and life-threatening medical issues for both of us. Sometimes, I felt like our lives were contained in someone's pinball machine with a maniac manning the flippers. And then a calmness would descend, and it felt like we were floating together in a sun-warmed blue lagoon. That last period of peacefulness was for two years, and then the pinball wizard took over, and nothing was ever the same again.

I now picture the pinball machine as broken and decrepit. I choose to not live inside it anymore. I can't float alone in the blue lagoon either, so I'm carefully maneuvering myself over the speed bumps and around the tree roots that spring up to trip me unawares. And somewhere in the distance, an orange aura is beckoning to me.

Chapter Twenty-Eight
Love Lives Forever

Lately, the phrase "love lives forever" seems to be popping up continuously in my peripheral vision. I believe this phrase because I believe love continues past this life into the next realm. Love stretches from my universe to you, Jerry, in God's heaven. It's not a stretchy substance like a rubber band or putty that we are each holding onto. It's more like Bluetooth. I send my thoughts to you, and you respond, although not always in a timely manner. Sometimes you must not be wearing your receiver. Maybe you are in airplane mode. I miss your rapid-fire, witty repartee responses. I still share things with you because I know I can, and because I believe it makes you happy, too, staying in contact with me. I feel your energy, and the vibration of your spirit emits warmth. Not like the furnace heat that poured off your body when we held each other for the last time. This is more like the warmth of a soft blanket caressing me just as I doze off for a nap.

When you are responding, I almost feel your touch like you have your hand on my shoulder or at the back of my neck. You always had the warmest hands. Maybe you have become a Reiki master and are treating me from a distance. Sometimes, I can walk into a room, and the scent of you is evident. These are rooms you never physically inhabited, but somehow your spirit evokes your familiar smell. Frequently, when I am thinking about you, the screen saver on my computer goes into hyperactive behavior. Or sometimes a large beautiful butterfly lingers near me for the longest time, resting on the yellow and red flowering lantana plant as I work on the patio. Is that you? Or sometimes, it's the hummingbird that whizzes alternately between me and the fuchsia-colored bougainvillea blooms. On rare occasions you fill the front yard with colorful quail—those beautiful little birds with their man buns bobbing as they run. We would always stop to watch them and found them so comical. I even named my company after them, Running Quail Press. In each case, I can feel your love cascading over me.

There are so many expressions about love. Love is a gamble. Love is for fools. Love is one-sided. Love is blind. Love means never having to say you're sorry (that one is a true fallacy). One of my favorites is "Love itself is what is left over when being in love has burned away, and this is both an art and a fortunate accident."

– Louis de Bernieries, *Corelli's Mandolin*

The other evening, Susanne Wilson, the Carefree Medium, autographed my copy of her new book, *Soul Smart*, and guess what she wrote? Love lives forever! Yes, Susanne, it does.

Chapter Twenty-Nine
If I Could Save Time...

I saw a story in the news recently where a dog tracked its owner, a dementia sufferer who had apparently wandered off, by a bottled scent. The bottle had been prepared two years previously and contained a gauze pad swabbed from the underarm of the dog's owner. It had been labeled and set aside for just this type of emergency. Hearing about this almost miracle made me think of the scents we associate with the people we love. Scents I miss and wish I could replicate.

I will always associate the scent of Canoe, an

inexpensive cologne readily available at drugstores throughout the land, with Jerry. When I leaned my head into the crook of his neck and inhaled his essence, he smelled spicy, masculine, comforting, and a little bit sexy. Months after he transitioned, I would sprinkle drops of this elixir on a cloth and tuck it in my pillowcase to soothe me as I fell asleep.

Every couple of years, our oak furniture required the application of several coats of Formby's tung oil to protect its gleaming finish. The astringent odor would linger in the house for days. Anytime I encounter it now, I immediately envision Jerry industriously applying it with a cloth to our treasured wood pieces.

The rich aroma of a bouquet of freshly cut and artfully arranged roses interspersed with delicate sweet peas often greeted me when I arrived home from work. And the recollection of us sitting on a white-painted bench in the backyard gorging ourselves on tree-ripened sweet juicy peaches or just-picked-off-the-vine Big Boy tomatoes raises waves of remembered smells of summer and hours of life-shaping conversations that lasted until twilight and mosquitoes drove us indoors.

I miss walking into the house in the evening and being greeted by a proffered tablespoon of sliced mushrooms sautéed in butter with fresh dill backed up by the heady smell of steak au poivre and roasted potatoes. Some people eat to live, and some of us live to eat. The fresh pungent smell of segmented oranges will always remind me of our final days together. It was the only food my husband would eat his last few days, when food no longer held any appeal. If I could save time in a bottle, it would be bottles of scents that I could open and have instant whiffs of our life together.

Chapter Thirty
Which First Holiday Hurts the Most?

∞

This is a trick question. Every holiday, every birthday, and every anniversary will be a first the year following your loss. And each one will cause you to ache a little with the memory of the last one you celebrated together. The last trip my soul mate and I took together was a short jaunt to Laughlin, Nevada, for a Valentine's Day getaway. I suggested we skip the trip since my spousal unit was scheduled to start radiation therapy the day after our return. He replied that he wanted to take his sweetheart away for the weekend. We always celebrated this heart-themed holiday with gifts, cards, and often a getaway. At lunch, earlier this week, another widow and I were discussing which holiday hurt the most the first year or two after our loss. She commented that Valentine's Day had hit her the hardest. When I asked why, she replied because they had never celebrated it. They had never exchanged valentines, given chocolates, or taken a romantic interlude on the holiday designated for lovers. She said she felt so sad they had missed the opportunity of celebrating Valentine's Day together during the twenty-four years of their marriage.

Thanksgiving was the first holiday I experienced without my husband. I was used to waking up to sounds of parade music coming from the television and the smells of stuffing being prepared, knowing soon a turkey would be roasting in the oven. I missed the friends and family who always joined us for the day. And the sounds of myriad conversations overlapping as we caught up on each other's lives. The pride I felt in our lovely home was shared with my kitchen-capable partner who would be busy cooking and serving our guests while telling stories, offering advice, and being the consummate host.

Some people avoid celebrating Christmas because they can't bear to participate in the festivities and possibly decorate a tree with the ornaments they chose together. The first Christmas after Jerry passed, Clo, her husband Johnny, and I determinedly put up the tree and hung the decorations. I placed twelve small cloisonné enamel heart ornaments on the tree. (I had purchased these at an after-Christmas sale the year before, and this was the first time they were displayed.) All of a sudden, each heart on the tree started spinning. My sister and I stared in delight and amazement. That was the only time the hearts spun. Each holiday has an impact and special memories.

When the second Christmas season came around, I knew I couldn't duplicate the past, but I wanted to see my friends, feed my friends, and share some holiday love. I planned an evening two weeks before Christmas and ordered full pans of lasagna from my favorite deli. Scented candles, mulled wine, and Christmas cookies filled the air with delicious smells. And that was the start of my new Christmas tradition.

Chapter Thirty-One
From Grief to Peace

My journey from grief to peace isn't over. I think my healing comes from making the journey. In the ten years since Jerry passed, major career changes have impacted my life. After losing my manufacturing company during the recession, I started an indie publishing company, Running Quail Press, where I enjoy helping and inspiring other writers to publish their books.

I also have a fun part-time gig as a customer service representative for a major retailer. It's a job I do from my home office, wearing whatever attire I feel like and even a hat as my whim dictates. I keep the background music low. Alexa does the DJ part, and I supply the caffeine. Sometimes I get calls from very sweet customers like seniors needing help placing their orders who tell me they weren't raised with computers. They delight in chatting about the kind of work they used to do. Or, I might talk with someone who lives alone and promised their pet a special weekend treat, which hasn't been delivered yet. We exchange the names of our pets and gain a little warmth from our conversation. Occasionally, I get a call that is so totally out of the blue, it must have been ordained by the universe. A young man had canceled an order for an item he had never selected or even admired. He said he was saving his money for something special. I told him that maybe he would receive that special item for husband-of-the-year award or birthday, anniversary, and Christmas gifts combined. He sighed and said he wasn't getting the husband-of-the-year award. I told him that you want your spouse to be your best friend and the person who always has your back. I went on to tell him about my friend who couldn't figure out why his marriage was failing when he always gave his 50 percent. I said in marriage you need to give 100+ percent, along with unconditional love and total respect. My new young friend was quiet for a moment and then said he could afford to do those things because they don't cost any money. He said he was still puzzled as to how he had placed his original order. I said that maybe the universe wanted us to talk today. He agreed with me, and we said goodbye. I think he might earn that husband-of-the-year award after all.

Another life change for me was that four years ago, I took a second long road trip, driving nearly 3,000 miles roundtrip from Arizona to Arkansas, to bring my sweet mother to live with me. My ninety-year-old mom, Jean, is also a widow. She brings immense joy and new challenges to my life.

We share a beautiful and rewarding mother-daughter friendship while she heroically battles numerous health issues, including lung cancer. Recently we have been remodeling our home, which has been an exciting experience and a great distraction from her medical issues.

I am happy and fulfilled most days through the love of God, family, friends, and work, but I always miss my Jerry.

Recently at church, I was asked to create a cardboard testimonial that challenged me to focus on my journey. For those unfamiliar, a cardboard testimonial is like a big sign. You write a brief message on each side of a large piece of cardboard. The front side typically states a personal struggle. The reverse side describes the deliverance from that struggle. The following is my testimonial:

(Front side) "Lost: Mobility, Spouse, Business & House."

(Reverse side) "I Never Lost God's Love."

During the process of researching and writing this book and while working on healing my own grief, I developed strong friendships with two very special women. I met Joy Collins and Cathy Marley several years ago when we were all members of a group called Women Writers of the Desert and were jointly published in *Love in Bloom: A Collection of Works by the Women Writers of the Desert*. Some of us liked to have an early lunch at the local Cheesecake Factory before our monthly meeting. Jerry enjoyed my writer friends and would sometimes join us. The group dissolved, but a few members including Joy, Cathy, and me stayed in touch, randomly meeting for lunch every few months. When Joy became widowed, I reached out to her, and we expanded our friendship. We shared lists of books that had been helpful and exchanged some long e-mails. Early on, we discovered many similarities in our marriages and the men we loved. We both knew we had married our soul mates. And we were both blessed to have Cathy for a friend. Cathy's first book, *Peeking Over the Edge* was published around the same time as Jerry's first novel, *Reversal of Fear*. Jerry and Cathy pooled resources on a couple of occasions and shared a bookseller table at local events. She stayed in touch with me by calling and making puppy play dates for our fur kids.

Over many lunches and meetings at Barnes & Noble, the three of us developed a project that we named "From Grief to Peace…a voice for those who mourn the loss of a soul mate." A joint book project morphed into three separate books, each written by one of us.

From www.FromGriefToPeace.org "Losing your soul mate can paralyze you with grief. Or it can send you frantically searching for answers, for ways to stop the pain of loss. Or both at the same time. Your soul mate is the person your heart and soul recognize to the depths of your being. At its core, a soul mate is only one thing – that one person in all the world who is "home" to your soul, the one you travel this life with, knowing they always have your back. They are your soft place to land. Losing that person to death is one of the most devastating things that can happen and leaves an emptiness as though you are missing half your heart."

"From Grief to Peace (FGTP) gives a voice to those who mourn the loss of a soul mate, empowering them and assisting them in their journey. This is a community where those who have lost their soul mate will find a holistic approach to healing and tools for persevering physically, financially, emotionally, and spiritually. By sharing our experiences with loss and healing, we want to help others transition from grief to peace in their own way and in their own time."

Principles of From Grief to Peace

1. I will allow myself to grieve my soul mate, knowing that this will be hard.
2. I will understand that I have the right to mourn the loss of my soul mate in my own way.
3. I will acknowledge that my grief has no timeline.
4. I will admit that grief has no rules.
5. I will feel comfortable standing up for myself when others put their expectations on me.
6. When I am stronger, I will pay it forward to help others who are mourning the loss of their soul mate. [1]

To learn more about From Grief to Peace, visit our website www.FromGriefToPeace.org or our Facebook community page From Grief to Peace.

[1] © From Grief to Peace, LLC, 2016, www.FromGriefToPeace.org, reprinted by permission.

Resources

Financial/Legal
Social Security Administration – SocialSecurity.gov

Physical
One Fit Widow – OneFitWidow.com

Emotional
Tom Zuba – TomZuba.com

From Grief to Peace – www.FromGriefToPeace.org

The Grief Toolbox – TheGriefToolbox.com

John Chuchman, MA, CDOS, Sacred Quest...growth through Loss and Love Workshops, Seminars, In-Service Programs, Retreats, and books On Grief, Caregiving, Church, and Spirituality, SacredTorch.com, poetman@torchlake.com

Spiritual
Mollie Morning Star, Evidential Psychic Medium – MollieMorningStar.com

Susanne Wilson, The Carefree Medium – CarefreeMedium.com

Books
Ain, Meryl, Fischman, Arthur M., and Ain, Stewart, *The Living Memories Project: Legacies That Last*, Little Miami Publishing Co, 2014

Anderson, George [medium], *We Don't Die*, Berkley, 2002 – GeorgeAnderson.com

Callanan, Maggie, and Kelley, Patricia, *Final Gifts*, Simon & Schuster, Reprint edition. 2012

Collins, Joy, *I Will Never Leave You: a soul mate's promise*, Desert Spirit Press, 2017 – JoyCollins.com

Davis Binsburg, Genevieve, M.S. *Widow to Widow*, Da Capo Press, Revised edition, 2004

Deits, Bob, M. Th, *Life after Loss*, Da Capo Press, Fifth Edition, 2008

Didion, Joan, *The Year of Magical Thinking*, Vintage, 2007

DuBois, Allison, [medium], *Don't Kiss Them Good-bye*, Touchstone, Reprint edition 2005 – AllisonDubois.com

Fatio, Bonnie Lou, *AgeEsteem: Growing A Positive Attitude Toward Aging*, Morgan James Publishing, 2007 – BonnieFatio.com

Fine, Carla, *No Time to Say Goodbye*, Main Street Books, Reprint edition, 2011

Guggenheim, Bill and Guggenheim, Judy, *Hello From Heaven*, Bantam, 2012 – After-Death.com

Hogan, R. Craig, PhD, *Your Eternal Self*, Greater Reality Publications, 2008, YourEternalSelf.com/drhogan2.htm

Holland, John [medium], *Born Knowing*, Hay House, 2003 – JohnHolland.com

Ireland, Mark, *Soul Shift*, Frog Books, 2011 – MarkIrelandAuthor.com

Kraft Thompson, Jill, *Finding Jill*, Mind, Body, and Soul Productions, Revised edition, 2013

LaMott, Anne, *Stitches*, Riverhead Books, 2013

Lewis, C.S., *A Grief Observed*, HarperOne, 2009

Marley, Cathy, *Breathing Again ...thoughts on life after loss*, CJM Press, 2017 – CathyMarley.com

McCalla, Betts, *Not Too Frayed to Fly: Surviving the loss of your soul mate*, Running Quail Press, 2017 – BettsMcCalla.com/

Meekhof, Kristin, LMSW and Windell, James, MA, *Widow's Guide to Healing*, Sourcebooks, 2015

Moody, Raymond, MD, *Life After Life*, HarperOne, Anv Spl edition, 2015 – LifeAfterLife.com

Neale, Walsch, Donald, *Conversations With God [Books 1, 2, and 3]*, Berkley, Box edition, 2005 and *Home With God*, Atria Books, Reprint edition, 2007 [about death] – NealeDonaldWalsch.com

Newton, Michael PhD, *Destiny of Souls*, Llewellyn Publications, 2 Sub edition, 2000 – Newton, Michael PhD, *Journey of Souls*, Llewellyn Publications, 1st edition, 1994

NewtonInstitute.org/about-tni/dr-michael-newton/

Noel, Brook and Blair, Pamela D., PhD, *I Wasn't Ready to Say Goodbye*, Sourcebooks, Updated edition, 2008

Rasmussen, Christina, *Second Firsts*, Hay House, Inc., 10.5.2013 edition, 2013

Redfield, James, *The Celestine Prophecy*, Warner Books, Inc. 1st edition, 1997 – CelestineVision.com

Sark, *Glad No Matter What*, New World Library, 2010, – PlanetSark.com/buy-stuff/sark-books/glad-no-matter-what/

Simpson, Virginia A. Ph.D., *What Grieving People Want You To Know* – DrVirginiaSimpson.com

van Lommel, Pim MD, *Consciousness Beyond Life*, HarperOne, Reprint edition, 2011, – PimVanLommel.nl/?home_eng

Van Praagh, James, Any books – VanPraagh.com

Weiss, Brian, Any books but especially *Many Lives Many Masters* – BrianWeiss.com

Wilson, Susanne, *Soul Smart What The Dead Teach Us about Spirit Communication*, Christine F. Anderson Publishing & Media; 2017 – CarefreeMedium.com

Zuba, Tom, *Permission to Mourn*, Bish Press, 2015 – TomZuba.com

Author's Profile

Betts McCalla is an indie publisher, speaker, and author residing in Peoria, Arizona. Brought up in the Midwest, she met the love of her life, Jerry, and they worked together as partners, producing local television shows in the Chicago area, including the counterculture *Underground News*.

Before she founded Running Quail Press, a local publishing firm for indie writers, Betts co-owned and managed a manufacturing company for years in southern California and Arizona. Her extensive writing career includes documentary television scripts, infomercial scripts, and articles for newspapers, including The Chicago Tribune.

After Jerry passed, Betts spent more than two

years reading, researching, and querying grief counselors, financial advisers, and medical personnel, trying to get questions answered and new problems resolved. She needed to gain clarity for the multitude of things she was experiencing physically, financially, and emotionally in her life, but she couldn't find what she needed in one book, five books, or even twenty. Two overfilled bookcases later, Betts decided to write *Not Too Frayed to Fly: Surviving the loss of your soul mate*, to offer practical guidance and give hope to people experiencing the loss of their soul mates.

Her passions include working to get rescue animals adopted, and supporting live music.

E-mail: betts.mccalla@runningquailpress.com